ACCOLADES

"*Relentless* is a page-turner... Natasha's a fabulous writer, I couldn't put it down... it's brilliant writing."

JACK CANFIELD
New York Times Best-Selling Author of the
Chicken Soup for the Soul series.

"Natasha Miller is a survivor, a kick-ass entrepreneur, and, now, a remarkable author. We have a lot to learn from her story and the challenges she's overcome. *Relentless is* a terrific read on leadership and business, yes, but it's also a blueprint for how to be a very special human being."

SCOTT OMELIANUK
Editor in Chief, *Inc. Magazine*

From a homeless teenager surviving in a youth shelter, to becoming a hugely successful entrepreneur, Natasha Miller is living proof that dedicated hard work and steely determination can elevate all of us. *Relentless* is a source of information and inspiration for every reader.

JAY FULCHER
CEO Zenefits

"Music saves lives. It saved Natasha Miller's. After getting dropped off at a homeless shelter on Christmas Day at age 16, chased out of her home by a nightmare mother, she used her violin and her singing to lift her out of grim circumstances and lead her to start a music production company that made lists of the fastest-growing companies in the country—a story Tasha tells with the same kind of unvarnished candor and heartfelt sentiment that always illuminated her beautiful singing."

JOEL SELVIN
#1 *New York Times* best-selling author
and music critic for the *San Francisco Chronicle*

"Natasha Miller's book hooked me within the first paragraph. The story of her life is told with such colorful description, it feels as if you are standing in the kitchen while her mom is trying to kill her. (What?) It's emotional, entertaining and informative. Natasha is one of the rare few. I am wowed!"

KIMBERLY FULCHER
Award-winning author and life coach

"*Relentless* is a beautiful and gripping story. You will not want to put it down! I laughed, I cried (sometimes at the same moment) and I felt inspired by the incredibly well written story by Natasha Miller. Natasha is living proof that dedicated hard work and steely determination can elevate all of us. *Relentless* is a source of information and inspiration for every reader."

CAROLINE LIND
2x Olympic Gold Medalist

"I met Natasha when I was the CEO of *Inc. Magazine* and she had just secured a place on the Inc. 5000, which means we'd identified her company, Entire Productions, as one of America's fastest growing. I could not have conceived that the confident, business-savvy entrepreneur standing before me had once been abandoned as a child, had faced tragedies that would have floored lesser beings and had also had an unrelated previous successful career in music. But all that, improbable as it seemed, is there in *Relentless*. Natasha's book—not to mention her amazing life—is a tribute to the redemptive power of art, friendship and entrepreneurship. Most of all, it's a tribute to the grit and creativity of a self-described "sad, anxious kid from the Midwest" who found a way. *Relentless* will stretch your concept of what is possible in life. Read it! You will not be able to put it down.

ERIC SCHURENBERG
CEO Mansueto Ventures
(Inc. Magazine and *FastCompany Magazine)*

"Natasha Miller is a force in every way—incredibly impressive even if you don't know what she's overcome. While *Relentless* starts by taking us into a surreal childhood that would have decimated others, it ends up showing us how to not only survive but also thrive. Surprising, inspiring and altogether unique, this is a story that stays with you long after your close the last page."

ANNA DAVID
New York Times bestselling author and
founder of Legacy Launch Pad Publishing

"*Relentless* is beautifully written and much of it feels as if you are sitting in a room listening to an old friend tell you stories about her childhood. The words flow naturally onto the page. I truly believe that Natasha's entrepreneurial spirit is what pushed her through the hardest of times. She was able to release music, manage gigs, start businesses, and raise her daughter all at once. Her ability to shift from one project to another and figure out how to make things work, especially through the Covid pandemic, is one hundred percent admirable. One of my favorite parts of the book is when Natasha describes her relationship with famous songwriter, Bobby Sharp. I felt like he became a grandfather figure to her and motivated her through stories of his own to reach for her goals.

Relentless is a book that any person can learn a great deal from. No one is without some kind of struggle, and if a sixteen-year-old homeless girl from Iowa can make it onto Inc.'s 5000 list of America's fastest-growing companies, then really, the sky is the limit."

KRISTI ELIZABETH
San Francisco Book Review

RELENTLESS

HOMELESS TEEN TO ACHIEVING THE ENTREPRENEUR DREAM

NATASHA MILLER

FOUNDER/CEO OF ENTIRE PRODUCTIONS,
3X INC. 5000 ENTREPRENEUR

WITH JAMIE BLAINE

Published and distributed by Poignant Press

Illustration by Amelia Noyes

Book cover design by Marcela Murillo

Author Photo by Valerie Carr

#beRelentless #RelentlessOnes

Library of Congress Control Number:

ISBN:
Paperback 979-8-985600-20-9
eBook 979-8-985600-21-6
Hardcover 979-8-9856002-2-3
Audiobook979-8-9856002-3-0

DEDICATION

For Bennett, who continues to help me rewrite my history.

DISCLAIMER

This book is a memoir. It reflects the author's present recollections of experiences over time and as recounted in her journals from 10 years of age, official transcripts, emails, texts and letters. Some names and characteristics have been changed, some events have been compressed, and some dialogue has been recreated.

TRIGGER WARNING

This memoir includes potentially disturbing and triggering content as outlined below. I encourage you to prepare yourself emotionally before proceeding in case reading it will be traumatizing for you.

- Self-Harm
- Verbal, Mental, Emotional Abuse
- Physical Abuse
- Child Neglect
- Depression
- Mental Illness
- Stillborn birth

CONTENTS

INTRODUCTION		13
PRELUDE	**WHAT CHRISTMAS MEANS TO ME**	17
CHAPTER ONE	**THE LITTLE GIRL FROM 29TH STREET**	27
CHAPTER TWO	**FAKE IT TILL YOU FIND YOUR WAY**	43
CHAPTER THREE	**RUN AWAY**	59
CHAPTER FOUR	**EMANCIPATION**	69
CHAPTER FIVE	**THE COURT AVENUE HUSTLE**	77
CHAPTER SIX	**FULL RIDE**	83
CHAPTER SEVEN	**EXIT, WEST**	95
CHAPTER EIGHT	**WELCOME, OLD SOUL**	103
CHAPTER NINE	**ALL IN**	113
CHAPTER TEN	**DEBUTS**	123
CHAPTER ELEVEN	**CREATE YOUR OWN STAGE**	133
CHAPTER TWELVE	**GAINING MOMENTUM**	143
CHAPTER THIRTEEN	**EMPTIEST NEST**	153
CHAPTER FOURTEEN	**BE THE CONDUCTOR WHEN YOU CAN**	159
CHAPTER FIFTEEN	**KEEPING SECRETS**	169
CHAPTER SIXTEEN	**DISGUISED OPPORTUNITIES**	181
CODA	**THE TAKEAWAY**	195
THANKS		199
ABOUT THE AUTHOR		201
APPENDIX		202
WORK WITH NATASHA		203
FOR BOOK CLUBS DISCUSSION + EXPERIENCE		209
BOOK CLUB QUESTIONS		211

INTRODUCTION

"The introduction may consist of an important chord or progression that establishes the tonality and groove for the following music, or they may be important but disguised or out-of-context motive or thematic material."

JAZZ COMPOSITION: THEORY AND PRACTICE

Hey, I'm Jamie. Co-writer and editor for *Relentless*.

The publishing industry can be quite the grind at times, and I confess to sometimes drowning in the ocean of empty words and vapid stories, fame sharks trying to monetize Tik Tok, wannabe influencers and self-help speakers desperate to build their brand. "Can't you send me something with some depth?" I begged my agent.

"How about helping an entrepreneur in San Francisco do a business book?" she asked.

"Like some slapdash pseudo-economic propaganda?" I groaned. "Ugh."

"Talk to her," she suggested. "What could it hurt?"

And that's how I met a funny, silly, somewhat insecure band nerd from Iowa, a nice Midwestern girl who had overcome a hellish childhood to become NorCal's hottest jazz chanteuse, founder of an award-winning company, speaker, educator, and business virtuoso.

Even this word-weary Nashville literary vet fell in love with her sweet, sad, messy story as we bonded over the joy of sarcasm, jokes about Beaverdale, math anxiety, the secret musical genius of Duran Duran, and the fact that, well, I'm also a former band nerd (ADHD drummer) who stayed in trouble for talking too much in class.

So, how did a scab-picking, anxiety-ridden, violin-obsessed lost girl find her way? Not simply to survive but lead, innovate, create and somehow rise above while staying true to her roots? The market is flooded with quick-fix bait and switch schemes, transcribed podcasts and recycled cliches on how to Win, Grow, Thrive, Find Your Passion/Purpose and Overcome—but we all know life is more complicated than that.

Dreams require sacrifice. But what is life without dreams? It takes sweat, blood and the grit to rise above, the willingness to get your ass kicked by life and show the hard-earned scars you got from fighting back.

Business book? Memoir? Self-help? Categories aren't important if the story is good. Dive in. Lose yourself in the pages.

Between the lines, you just might find the inspiration to keep pushing on.

As we finished Relentless, I had one request. "A book is kinda like a concert, y'know. So would it be okay if I introduce you to the stage?"

"Really?" she said.

Please make welcome, my friend, Natasha Miller.

JAMIE BLAINE
Author, *Midnight Jesus* and *Mercy Never Sleeps*
Nashville, Tennessee, 2022

For a more immersive experience, go to
theRelentlessBook.com/unlock.
This site was created for you to reference
and enjoy while reading the book.

WHAT CHRISTMAS MEANS TO ME

DES MOINES, IOWA. CHRISTMAS, 1987

"I'm going to fucking *kill* you!" my mother screams, punctuating her threat with a twelve-inch butcher knife.

I snap back, giving her a quick once-over. Rail-thin and haggard, hip bones poking through faded jeans. Thick, frizzy brown hair pulled back by bobby pins, the stench of cigarettes and cinnamon on her breath. She smokes a pack of Camel Lights a day, chasing each hard drag with Coke on ice and wads of Big Red gum. Caffeine, nicotine, sugar—this is what fuels the hurricane of chaos and rage that is my mom.

I don't know what I did wrong. We'd been cutting up day-old bread to make stuffing for Christmas dinner and maybe I was slicing the chunks too big or too small or smiling too much or not enough. Doesn't take much to set her off.

We're having guests over for dinner, a huge deal for us, and despite the tension, I cannot help but feel some sort of hope that we will finally have a Christmas marked by those things: hope, joy, family, togetherness. You know, like those shows you see on TV.

My boyfriend is coming. Phillip is my first true love. Straight-A maker, D&D fan, can play "Moonlight Sonata" on the choir room's upright piano and make it sound like a Bösendorfer grand. Phillip comes from a "good" family, so his mother thinks I'm not worthy of her youngest son. But he defies her and sees me anyway. When you're sixteen, rebellion just makes romance that much more exciting. I'd seen enough John Hughes movies to know that.

Do moms in John Hughes movies wield butcher knives?

Truth is, it's not the first time she's hurled the words *I'm going to fucking kill you* at me. But this time feels different. Or maybe I'm just fed up. My therapist said I should start standing up to her threats.

The knife edge gleams in the kitchen light. I breathe deep and hold my ground. Her eyes go wild. That's when I run.

She chases me from the kitchen to the living room, waving the blade and cursing as a hundred tiny lights twinkle from our tree.

Well, that's it, I think, as my mother slams me against the wall. *So much for my sweet, fantasy TV Christmas.*

"Linda…," Dad says.

Dad and my little brothers are over by the Christmas tree. He never sticks up for me, so I'm not surprised when his only response to Mom chasing me with a knife is a weak, pleading mention of her name. Dad loves me and he's always there to listen. I don't understand why he can't or won't protect me from her.

My mom responds by grabbing and shoving me as I attempt to get away. "I'm gonna throw you through this fucking window!" she growls while shaking me, her long, manicured nails digging into my neck.

The large pane of glass is the frame for the gorgeous magnolia tree that bursts with flowers in the spring and drips with icicles at this time of the year.

I pull loose and dash up the stairs, ducking into my bedroom and locking the door with its skeleton key. Heart pounding, I grab the phone and stare at the touch tone buttons, stabbing the numbers in succession. **NINE. ONE.…**

I've held this phone so many times, staring at the numbers, pressing the first two, losing my nerve. You don't call the cops. Not for situations like this. You just don't. But I can't live this way anymore. With shaky fingers, I punch the final digit.

ONE.

"Emergency 9-1-1. What is your location?" the voice on the line asks.

"My mom is trying to kill me," I say quietly.

"I'm sorry, I can't hear you?"

Scared that she might be listening, I whisper slightly louder. "My mom said she's going to kill me, please help me," I beg, quickly reciting my address.

No one comes upstairs to check on me. Not my brothers, not even my dad. I'm sure he hopes the drama is over. I'm still shaking and my brain spins. I start to feel dizzy. *Will somebody really come to help?*

Minutes later, my father's strained voice echoes up the stairs. "Linda, the police are here," he says, sounding surprised. I peek out my bedroom window. Two police officers walk up our front step, boots crunching on the ice.

I crack my door so I can try to hear what they're saying, worried that I've somehow made a terrible situation worse. *What's going to happen to me? Will they cuff my mother and throw her in the back of the police car?*

I'm torn between fear and relief when my dad's voice breaks the silence. "Tash," he calls. "Come down here."

The officers are looming, thumbs in gun belts, looking me over as I creep down the stairs. *They won't arrest me—right?* The needle swings back from relief to stark fear. Thankfully, my mom is nowhere in sight.

The taller officer peppers me with questions.

Can you show me your arms? Are you bleeding anywhere else? Look up to the ceiling so I can see your neck. Is anything broken? What happened here today?

They study my scrapes and cuts. I can sense my mother's presence nearby. The stakes are higher now. If she was threatening to stab me or push me out a window before....

Please, God, do not leave me here with her, I pray.

The policemen swap glances. "I'm sorry, sir," the tall cop tells my dad. "There's really nothing we can do. Your daughter's injuries aren't severe enough for us to arrest your wife and we can't do anything for your daughter." He pauses. Dad nods. Panic sears me and my heart leaps back into my throat.

"However," the officer says, "there is a place you can take her if you feel she's in danger." He hands my father a business card with large capital letters on the front: "Y.E.S.S." Dad takes the card and closes the door. My mom is watching. I can feel it.

"Tash," Dad says, "Go pack some of your things. Right now."

He rushes into the kitchen and returns with a Hefty trash bag. I haul it to my room and frantically begin to fill it up. The Christmas presents I'd unwrapped earlier, a few pieces of my favorite clothes, *Ethan Frome*, by Edith Wharton. A package of Hostess Ho Hos someone from church choir youth group gave me during our White Elephant gift exchange game.

Do I bring my violin? Surely, I won't be at the shelter that long. *Will I?* I pluck the low string and stare at the woodgrain, varnish fading from the constant pressure of my hands and chin.

Music is my lifeline. My life. Music is blood. I'm classically trained, first violin section of school orchestra and sing in the choir at church. I play in the Des Moines Youth Symphony, too. I've been working on the Bach *Partita No. 2 in D minor*. The symphony concert isn't until after winter break but it's a difficult solo piece and I'm worried about getting my practice in.

I catch my reflection in the mirror on my closet door. I'm dressed in a gray wool matching sweater/pants set from the Gap. It's the nicest outfit I own. Makes me feel sophisticated and grown. *It's Christmas. Phillip was coming. Today was supposed to be good.*

"Tash, come on," my father calls, snapping me out of my daydream. I slide the case back under my bed. A couple of days without practice won't hurt.

I head out front, load the trash bag into the back of our Mazda GLC wagon, and climb inside where Dad and my brother Justin are waiting. "GLC" stands for Great Little Car, but the Mazda is a rusted-out rattletrap with a muffler dragging sparks. It also backfires at the most inopportune times, sounding like gunshots ringing down our street. This does not help my self-esteem.

We drive in silence past piles of dirty, grey snow and head downtown. I have no idea what to expect. My mind flip-flops, anxiety to hope, imagining some swank old mansion filled with kids like me and a kind, motherly figure who listens to our stories, offering comfort and hope.

But wait—what if it sucks even worse than home?

Dad swings the wagon into the lot. One lone light shines from the building's bland facade. The sign below the light reads **Y.E.S.S** and in smaller letters below, *Youth Emergency Shelter Service*. We hurry to the door. It's freezing, and in the madness of getting out of the house, I forgot my coat.

A shelter representative meets us at the door. He talks to Dad a moment before inviting me inside. Justin follows behind me. "I'm afraid the young man can't come in with you," the shelter rep says. "In fact, why don't you all just say your goodbyes here?"

A look of confusion and sadness flashes over my little brother's face. He shouldn't have to be here, watching his big sister get locked in a shelter on Christmas Day. I throw my arms around him. "I'm sorry," I say, both of us crying, "So sorry."

My dad stands by, quiet. It's harder to tell what he is thinking. Just doing what he's told, I guess. Might even be a relief for him. We nod and exchange an awkward look. The door closes and they are gone.

I walk into the shelter. Everything is a yellow haze in the flickering florescent lights. It's sparsely furnished with mismatched crappy furniture that looks like it's been salvaged from garage sales and government auctions. Through the foyer, there's a den where a handful of teens are watching *Dukes of Hazzard* on a giant old console television. The antenna is broke, and the static makes Bo Duke look like he's driving the General through a snowstorm.

The teens turn as I step into the room. "Hey, look, she's so *preppy!*" one of them cracks. They all start to laugh, and I realize I must look ridiculous to them. The kids here are all in tattered, out-of-fashion jeans and stretched-out tees. They look like street kids, runaways. The heat of embarrassment burns through me as they look me up and down, but I avoid their eyes.

What the hell am I doing here?

The shelter rep says his name is Steven. He shows me to a room where I meet my roommate, Tracy. "Hey," I say. "I'm Tasha."

She stares through me with cold, dead eyes. Her blonde hair is dirty and matted. I wonder if this sad girl even got to celebrate Christmas at all. I brought my new purple plaid flannel blouse, so I dig it out of the bag.

"I got this for Christmas," I tell her. "But you can have it."

I hand it to her, hoping it might break the ice. Maybe we'll bond through trouble and be friends and tell each other the crazy story of how we landed in the teen shelter on Christmas night.

"Thanks," Tracy says with zero emotion and eyes on the floor. She stuffs the blouse into a rickety drawer and disappears into the TV room.

I pull my stuff out of the trash sack, clinging to a little bag of miniature versions of candy that Phillip bought me from 7-Eleven a few days before. Tootsie Rolls, Chic-O-Sticks, banana Laffy Taffy. York Peppermint Patties are my favorite, and I often lie in bed, binging on sweets until my anxiety melts away.

I burn through a few York patties and try to sleep but my mind won't let me rest. I think about dreams of a big, family Christmas, squeezing Phillip's hand under the table as everyone makes a mad dash to pile food on their plates. About my mom's sudden threat, the long blade shining in the kitchen light, Christmas tree twinkling as her nails gouged my neck. Not hot pink or fuchsia neon frost nails, a tasteful shade of beige nude, meticulously manicured.

My mother might be bat-shit crazy, but she's a bit exotic and much hipper than the other moms on our street. Sometimes, that makes me desperate for her acceptance even more. I am not hip. Even in my matching Gap ensemble. I am a classical-violin-playing, scab-picking, anxiety-ridden freak, freaking out and trying to sleep in a rundown shelter for troubled teens.

Merry Christmas. Life is so fucking weird.

CHAPTER ONE

THE LITTLE GIRL FROM 29TH STREET

"HER LIFE"

I grew up on 29th Street, just on the eastern edge of the nicer neighborhoods in Des Moines, Iowa. Our neighborhood was fairly normal and most of the kids seemed to have happy, carefree lives, so I spent a lot of time living vicariously through them.

The Cusanos were a big Catholic family who lived next door. They were strict, but unless you consider chores to be a form of child abuse, there was nothing inappropriate going on.

Rumors circulated of a fierce wooden paddle used to smack the behinds of naughty Cusano kids, but I suspect they learned good behavior early on.

Vicky Cusano was a year older. She had curly red hair and could be kind of mean but eventually she warmed up to me, even though I already had a reputation as the weird kid on our block. Now and then, I'd get to spend the night over at Vicky's. Her mom was a little scary but still, those nights away from home were like escaping Alcatraz.

Sometimes we'd crash on the living room floor in sleeping bags, watching Mork from Ork wreak havoc at McConnell's Music Store, befriending young violinists and zapping mannequins to life. Other times, Vicky and I would sleep in the attic. (That's where Mork lived!) Loved it. The Cusano kids used their attic space as a bunkhouse/playroom with toys, records, posters, and clothes scattered everywhere.

The Cusanos also had the only swing set on our block, with a teeter-totter, stiff plastic swings and a big metal slide that would scorch your backside on a hot summer day. Back behind the swing set there was a shed with a refrigerator where they stored the groceries it took to sustain a family of six.

I'd sneak over and steal a Hostess cupcake or one of those individual apple fruit pies. Vicky's dad was a janitor and her mom babysat, so I could not understand why they had so much more than we did. Maybe that's how I justified theft. I was petrified that Mama Cusano might catch me and threaten me with the heat of angry Jesus, but that sweet, sugary rush was worth the risk.

Vicky's family shared a lake house with relatives, and once a year I was invited to come along. I'd ride on the floor in the back of the van, wedged between cases of Shasta soda and stacks of marshmallows and hot dogs. The cabin was on a bluff with steep stairs leading down to the dock. It was a bit rustic and worn, but to me—totally exquisite. I loved to stand at the water's edge smelling boat fuel and barbeque, that peaceful feeling staring out over the waves.

The Cusanos had a speedboat, and the whole family loved to water ski. Well, everybody but me. In Kindergarten, one of the neighborhood moms rounded up the young kids and hauled us to the Roosevelt High pool so the teenagers could teach us to swim. Their method was simple, but cruel. Drag me to the deep end and dunk me under three times. I was so traumatized by the experience that I wouldn't learn to swim until nearly three decades later.

I loved riding in the Cusano's speedboat, though. Cool wind rushing through my hair as water splashed against the sides of the boat. We'd hit a wave and I'd go weightless, flying up into the air. Awesome! Sometimes I'd strap on a lifejacket and wade out into the shallows. For the most part, no one made fun of me. At least not to my face.

When I was four, the family at the corner house invited me to play in their kiddie pool. I rushed to ask my mother if I could go. My mom took a long pull off her Camel and sighed, "Yeah, I guess."

I ran to get my swimsuit. She grabbed me and put me in a chair. "Sit still!" she said. "I'm going to put your hair up first."

She jerked my hair, twisting it into a tight bun on the top of my head. I started crying, which only made my mom pull that much harder, anger radiating from her eyes. But it was just another day with my mother, and I knew that soon enough, I'd be on my way to freedom and fun. So, suck it up and get it over with. I ran fast as my little legs would carry me, bare feet on a summer sidewalk, threadbare towel in tow.

Jess and Deb lived in the house on the corner. Their mom, Charlene, was friends with mine, and some nights, my parents would go over to their house to play cards.

Charlene was a simple, stable, no-nonsense mom. Cute and tiny, she kept her hair short, wore big plastic glasses and would sometimes flash a smile that showed a softer side. When it was freezing out, she'd drive us all to school and pick us up. You never had to wonder if Charlene would be there. I used to wish that she could be my mom too.

The Long family lived across the street and boy, were they strange. The grandmother lived with them and would sit on the front porch glaring at all the kids like some old devil witch. In fact, that's what we used to call her.

Hey, Ol' Devil Witch is giving you the eye. I bet she's thinking about cooking you in a big pot with some carrots.

Shut up! She's gonna cook you first!

None of us kids ever dared to go in that house. But the two youngest Long kids would sometimes join us to play Freeze Tag or Truth or Dare or catch lightning bugs in the vacant field as the sun went down in early summer.

Everybody knew that my mom was crazy. When the weather was mild, we left the doors and windows open and the whole neighborhood could hear her screaming and calling me "bastard," saying how much she hated me. It was shameful but down deep, in some secret way, I prayed she'd scream so loud that someone would hear her, and I'd be saved. If people knew, someone would surely step in. Right?

Maria Long was a few years older and one day, she came up with a plan. Her uncle knew a policeman, so she told him about my mom.

Oh my God... it's happening! Someone is going to come to rescue me.

I was so filled with hope after Maria told me about her uncle's policeman friend. Every night, I closed my eyes and thought, *this is the last day . . . this is the last day....*

You would have thought angels were coming to fly me away to Fantasy Island. Every night. Night after night.

Until finally, I realized, *no one is coming.*

My father had wide, expressive eyes with a swoop of black hair and a beard like the king on a playing card. I didn't blame him for allowing Mom to abuse me. It never occurred to me that everyone else probably did, wondering why he wouldn't stand up to her. To me, it felt like he was stuck in the same storm as the rest of us. Somehow, he couldn't find a way out, for me or himself.

Dad seemed solid as a rock. He cared about all the little details of my life, hopes and dreams, who my friends were, all my failed attempts to get the attention of various boys. Dad was smart too, helping with homework, reading my poetry and offering praise.

Every night after dinner, we would drive down to Dahl's grocery store and I would beg him to divorce Mom. Weekends were the best because my dad was home with us. He would wake up in the morning and cook scrambled eggs and hash browns with bacon. We'd also get blueberry muffins, and although they came in a box from Dahl's, they were *soooo* moist with fat chunks of sweet berry in every bite. My brothers and I would lick our fingers and dot the plate, scavenging every crumb.

Dad spent lots of time with my brothers too, participating in all their sports activities. Whether hockey, soccer or baseball, they were natural athletes early on. Before games, you could find Dad mowing the field at Raccoon Valley, the local baseball diamond. He never missed a game.

Even Mom seemed to adore my brothers with their cute bowl-cuts and cherub faces. She made and packed their lunches, but never much of the other "mom" stuff like making sure they took a bath or brushed their teeth. Mom never helped with homework or asked how their day went or anything like that. Dad tried to do double duty and I filled in best I could. I wanted to be a good big sister, but it was tough with Mom always on my case.

I never saw my parents show affection to one another. They didn't hug or kiss or hold hands. They didn't even sleep in the same room. Sometimes, they would argue at night but for the most part, they lived as if the other didn't exist.

After we went to bed, my mother would plug her headphones into the stereo and zone out for hours, smoking cigarettes and listening to Linda Ronstadt records late into the night.

My bedroom was next to hers but still managed to be a sanctuary. Aunt Susan had handed her old twin bed down to me. It had turned oak posts on the headboard, and I also got her oak dresser and a child-sized table with chairs. This was enough to create a make-believe world where I could block out the present and lose myself in dreams and plans of better days to come.

I would rearrange my room to take me someplace magical and safe. Sometimes it was a fancy hotel in a distant city, other times a sprawling library filled with tall mahogany shelves and mysterious books, or a radio station, where I would pretend to be a DJ, listened to, loved, semi-famous and sending songs out into the night.

My bedroom walls were cracking, and sometimes the plaster would start to crumble and fall. I would make a concoction from glue, flour and water to spackle and patch the places that were falling apart. Then I began adding color to the mix and soon enough the walls of my bedroom became my very own art gallery made up of drawings in marker, crayon, and pen. When friends came over, I'd get them to sign my wall.

But I wasn't popular, so I didn't have that many friends. And I didn't get to have sleepovers either. So, there weren't a lot of signatures on my wall—but the few that I did have, well, I thought that was really cool. My brothers added their names to my wall too, but they were more into skateboards and Hulkamania than artistic endeavors.

For all my mom's rage, I never got in trouble for that wall. It was one of the few places I felt like I could express myself and be me. My art wall was one small win in a torrent of suck.

With books, I could escape to another world, far from my own. *Tuck Everlasting, Ramona the Pest.* Judy Blume and the weird wonder of *Grimm's Fairy Tales.* I would have given anything to be Thumbelina or Princess from *Princess and the Pea.*

Aunt Susan gave me the complete *Little House* collection and I devoured all nine, tucked under my covers, paperback an inch from my face, pretending to be Laura Ingalls as she explored the wilderness of Walnut Grove.

I figured out a way to read into the night without my parents knowing, learning the sound of their individual footsteps, the cadence and weight that makes each unique. Dad's footsteps were heavy on the stairs. I knew I was safe if he were coming up to check on us or go to the bathroom.

But if I heard the rabbit-thump of Mom's soft, quick steps, I would jerk the string that I'd tied to my ceiling fan's pull-chain and snap off the lights.

Justin and Jeremy shared bunk beds and would sneak into my room when we were all supposed to be asleep. I would pretend to be Johnny Carson, hosting *The Tonight Show*, interviewing my brothers about toys and sports and the silly, fun stuff of kid imaginations. We would slap our hands over our mouths to hold in the laughter as it spilled out in snorts from our noses. You never dream you'll remember those seemingly insignificant moments so fondly for the rest of your life.

My room was a mess, old clothes and books piled from table to bed. One day when I was about eight, my mom came blazing in, screaming and thrashing about, kicking whatever was in her path. I had an antique tin dollhouse and Mom booted it hard as she could, putting a huge dent into the side.

I shrank back into the corner, terrified. Why was she willing to ruin a precious antique just to let out her anger? She'd spent a lot of time scavenging yard sales and antique shops to find that dollhouse.

Why does she hate me so much? What did I do? And why does everyone else in this house act like this is normal?

"Get out of my house!" she shouted. "I don't *ever* want to have to look at your ugly face again!"

I threw a bunch of clothes into my Holly Hobbie sleeping bag and started down the stairs. Where would I go? Could the Cusano kids hide me in their attic for a few days? Would Maria Long help me out? I know! I'll go to Charlene's, my dream replacement mom.

Despite my fear, the thought of escape was tantalizing. *Anywhere's gotta be better than here.* The thrill of freedom was short-lived when Mom saw me coming downstairs with my bag.

"Get your ass back in that room, you little bitch," she hissed. I turned and headed back up as she screamed hatred and threats. Dad was at work and hopefully, my little brothers were somewhere playing where they could not hear her voice.

I dumped my Holly Hobbie bag out on the floor, crashed face down on my bed and cried.

Huddled in my room, I would pick at my skin until it festered. Once dried over, this became an intense project of picking and lifting so the scab would come off and blood or puss would emerge. Picking scabs kept my anxious mind occupied. It was a goal to achieve, a meticulous practice.

A rush of endorphins would flood through me when I pulled off a scab. I loved the touch of that rough, red piece of crust. Cool air on a bright hot wound, blood oozing. Here, I could control the pain, focusing it into one fiery scrape on my arms or legs or chest, turning up the volume loudly enough to drown out the pain inside. Once I had gouged open the wound, the process of healing and picking could start all over again.

Like cutting for other kids, my scab routine offered both sweet relief and gut-wrenching shame. Once, I dug out a spot on my right buttock, bigger and deeper than before. The blood would seep into my cotton underwear, and I'd hide them under my mattress, scared that someone might discover my awful secret.

My mother didn't clean our rooms or do laundry, so my father must have found my underwear, because they always returned clean. And if my dad found them, then he must have known. But if he knew, he never said a word.

Anxiety stirs fear. Fear amplifies anxiety. The sludge swirls, thicker and toxic in your chest. *Pick, pick, pick.*

Other than my room, one of the few safe havens I had was my Grandmother Miller's house. She lived in a beautiful white Colonial on a tall green hill, over in the nice part of town. A large parkway sat just across the street and there was a creek where my brothers and I could play. During the winter, we would sled down the hill on saucers and get into snowball fights.

Grandma Geraldine had the wit and intuition of an artist. She was whip-smart, fun, and rich. Or at least she sure seemed rich to me.

We'd play dress-up in her elegant clothes and she'd let me smear Coty "New Real Orange" Lipstick across my lips and teeth. We danced and sang Rosemary Clooney's "Buckle Down Winsocki" while eating frosted animal crackers and watching *Carol Burnett.*

Grams introduced me to Joan Baez. (Not in person. Just her music.) "Honest Lullaby" was my favorite. I used to sing that song about padded bras and jocks hiding their vernal equinoxes in faded jeans. I was forty before I figured out what Baez meant by "vernal equinox." Did Grandma know we were singing about a college boy's erection?

Actually, yeah. She probably did. Grams and I were thick as thieves.

Even though she was a highly respected member of St. Theresa's. Grams had gay friends, believed that Catholics should let priests marry, and that women should be able to wear the collar and give homilies, too. I'm not sure if the thought "God is a Woman" ever came to her mind but given more time, I'm sure that it would have.

Grams authored five books with titles like *Help your Child for Life* and *Family Communications: Keeping Connected in a Time of Change.* She taught self-esteem workshops to the women prisoners at Mitchellville Detention Center and by letting me help by setting up and passing out worksheets, boosted my own as well. She spoke to groups about the importance of healthy communication within the family and sometimes I would even appear in the educational filmstrips that were commissioned by her publisher, Paulist Press, a Catholic institution established by missionaries in 1858.

Yep, you read that right. My grandmother taught people about the importance of family connection and self-esteem while her daughter-in-law beat me down and called me "worthless bitch." Dad even shot and produced the films. That's some heavy irony right there.

But if Grams had any insight, she didn't offer it to Dad. I don't know if he could've taken advice from her anyway. Often, it's easier to help a stranger than your own flesh and blood. Grandma Miller grew up in a dysfunctional house too, with a stern, ultra-conservative dad. Then she married a raging alcoholic. But Grams was raised staunch Catholic. Keep your secrets. With all the shit she went through, it's amazing that she came out as well as she did.

One time, Grandma had my father take a photo to use in one of her educational films of Mom and me sitting back-to-back on the big rock at the bottom of the hill. We sat, barely touching, arms crossed, the air around us glowing with hate. Was it supposed to be symbolic somehow? Is that why she had us sit facing away from each other?

People forget that in the early eighties, counseling wasn't really a thing. Denial ruled the day. You might have a guidance counselor at school, but private therapy was something on TV, like Bob Newhart, a place for rich housewives to vent and refill their Valium scripts. We had no Oprah or Dr. Phil butting in and "decent" people didn't discuss their feelings in public.

But Grams knew what was going on between me and my mom because I told her. So did Dad. Even my Uncle Kevin mentioned it to her a few times. But back then, you just didn't talk outside of family about problems like that. Unless my mother stuck my hands on a hot stove burner or left me bleeding in the street, things were okay.

Every night, my dad would come home from work and go straight up to the piano room. He'd sit at our shiny black Baldwin upright and play ragtime, pop and classical until dinner was ready. Sometimes in counterpoint, other times harmony, weaving a beautiful and fluid pastiche in his own self-taught style. I would sit right next to him on the piano bench, watching his fingers glide over the keys. That's how I learned to play, watching and listening, plinking out high notes to compliment his song.

Eventually, I started singing along. "Misty" was the first song Dad taught me. From a vocal perspective, Ella Fitzgerald is jumping in the deep end of the pool, but I *loved* it, notes floating over the melody, lightness and dark, the way a song can take you someplace other, out of yourself and away.

I would stare out the front window, waiting for my father's car to pull into the drive. That was our time, just the two of us, a capsule of peace and safety, music all around. My mom never bothered us when we were in the piano room. Every day, we would hide up there and sing until she called us down to eat. Music was my refuge.

Dinner was usually casserole or spaghetti, or my mother's specialty, pork fried rice. She was a decent cook but I couldn't stand those slimy peas or green beans so we'd play that old charade where I couldn't leave the table until I finished all my food. Sometimes I'd be stuck there for over an hour while my brothers went out to play. I would hide the beans or spit them in a napkin. Every now and then, I'd just choke them down and be done with it. Once, she came at me with a heavy wooden spoon and smacked me hard as she could on the back of my arm.

"I'm gonna kill you," she seethed. "I'd rather kill you and go to jail than have to look at your face one more day."

Once dinner was over, I would fetch Dad's heavy pewter mug from the freezer so he could have his beer. He'd buy at least a six-pack of Budweiser on our nightly trips to Dahl's Grocery and drink them after dinner, cracking the pop-top with a mighty hiss, that golden stream glug-glug-glugging down into the frosty mug.

I never saw him drunk. His personality didn't change. I imagine he sat there, drinking one beer after another, and contending with his past (*alcoholic father, distant mom*) and present. (*demanding job, out-of-control wife, three kids who need someone to take up the slack.*)

My dad slept on the couch. I don't ever remember him and Mom sharing a bed or a room or much of anything. I guess he would watch TV and drink his six-pack, maybe more, moving to the couch when the liquor let him forget his problems long enough to sleep.

Late at night, I would sneak from my room, creep down the stairs—careful to avoid the creaky ones—and lay on the floor beside him. It felt safer than being upstairs in the room next to my mom, especially after she'd had an episode. Sometimes my dad's hand would flop off the edge of the couch and I would reach up and hold his fingers until I fell asleep.

The nightmares would come, even there. I was tiny, like Thumbelina, and the world was huge and looming, giant people, giant tables and chairs, all waiting to crush me. Before long, the dream would startle me back awake. My father would be snoring, arm laid over his eyes. I felt bad for him, though at that age, I couldn't articulate why.

Even the couch he slept on was a dirty family secret. We threw our trash behind it until it heaped up in piles, spilling out from the sides. Cigarette butts and gum wrappers, greasy napkins, lollipop sticks. I don't know why we lived like Oscar the Grouch. I was ashamed of our behavior, and I felt trapped, but I did it too.

When I turned ten, I started keeping a journal. Emotions look different when you get them out of your head and my feelings didn't take up as much space inside when I put them down on paper.

And with emotions not so overwhelming, I found the space for something new.

CHAPTER TWO

FAKE IT TILL YOU FIND YOUR WAY

"YOU'RE A NATURAL"

In fourth grade, when I was ten, a music teacher named Mr. Carlson came to Perkins Elementary for an all-school assembly. He had mossy brown hair that he wore in a comb-over and was dressed in a drab polyester suit. Mr. Carlson held up a violin and said he was looking to recruit students for free lessons. He played a few bars that impressed us all then asked, "Can I have a volunteer?" lifting the violin higher. "Who wants to give it a try?"

I thrust my hand into the air. Kids across the auditorium did the same. Somehow, out of hundreds of outstretched hands, he chose mine.

I walked to the front and placed the violin under my chin as the teacher instructed. He positioned my fingers around the frog of the bow and placed it against the strings. With a nod from him, I pulled the bow back and the strings came to life.

"You're a natural!" Mr. Carlson exclaimed.

I rushed home after school to tell my parents the news. "I got chosen to play the violin in school!" I gushed. "They give you an instrument and I get to take lessons for free!"

Actually, my school had a whole inventory of instruments for any student who wanted to learn. Still, out of a whole gymnasium full of kids —my entire school—the music teacher picked me! They would give me a violin! And lessons! For free!

That was close enough to a miracle for me.

I mean, sure, I played piano from my dad's lap and could sing a few songs, but now I had an instrument that was uniquely and completely my own. The teacher said I was already good.

I started lessons right away and progressed quickly. Best part, I could take the violin home, not only to practice but also to play along with my dad.

Soon, we were up in the piano room performing duets, my dad making piano arrangements for the practice pieces I brought home from school. My father didn't just play by ear, he could read music too, even complicated classical movements. I began to pass him up though, and before long, he was learning about music from *me*.

Music has the capacity to go beyond words, and my dad and I began to communicate through our sessions. I could sense how proud he was of me, the way my ability leveled the ground between us in the piano room. Or *music* room, rather, I should say.

Mr. Carlson taught me using the Suzuki books, but I really didn't know how to read anything above an *e* on the staff. Mostly, I learned to play by ear, basically faking my way through my first violin concerto, Vivaldi's "Concerto in A minor." He would play various passages from the sheet music and for the most part, I simply copied what I heard.

If Mr. Carlson knew I was faking, he didn't seem to care because he kept giving me little round stickers that said GOOD JOB. Some of the stickers were the scratch and sniff kind that smelled like strawberries or hot chocolate. My favorite was buttered popcorn. I kept those books with the stickers on the front and if I close my eyes, I can still smell the popcorn.

Our backyard was covered with overgrown, unruly trees, weeds, and old junk cars that my father had plans to fix someday, so during the summer, my mother would lay out in the front.

One day, I was in the yard while my mom was tanning on her plastic lounge chair, flipping every half-hour, when the radio DJ would call out to those baking in the sun. She always wore a bikini, misting her brown skin with water from a spray bottle before slathering Bain du Soleil over her slender arms and legs, the smell of suntan lotion and fresh-cut grass after a late-night storm filling the air.

Some kids came to our gate and I was excited, hoping they'd ask me to play. My mom walked over and offered us a pack of saltine crackers. She had never offered me anything, much less to the children in our neighborhood. I basked in that moment, hoping she'd turned a corner, deciding to do better and not be so angry all the time, but before the day was over, she was screaming at me again.

A few months later, she took me to the 5-7-9 at Merle Hay Mall. 5-7-9 was a popular clothes store for tweens in that size between kids and adults. My mom was in a good mood that day, lighthearted, a skip in her step. We browsed the clothes at 5-7-9 and she bought me a few things.

The kids at school wore pink Izod polos with Calvin Klein's but I was used to K-Mart jeans and itchy sweaters from DAV Thrift. I would pray some classmate didn't notice that I was wearing their thrift store hand-me-downs. So, I was beyond thrilled to get brand-new clothes from a cool place in the mall.

We left the store. My mom started walking fast. I got a stitch in my side and couldn't keep up. She turned back, yelling, cutting me in public with her harsh words. I should have known her kindness wouldn't last. She just couldn't keep it up that long.

But if my mother was capable of even a few moments of random kindness, maybe there was hope. Besides, it was too late. I already had that 5-7-9 bag in my hand.

At a routine check-up, the doctor listened to my heart longer than usual. "Interesting…," he said, before telling my dad I'd have to see a cardiologist.

The cardiologist was an Indian man, gentle, but difficult to understand due to his thick accent. He explained that I had a rare heart condition called pulmonary valve stenosis that might require open-heart surgery. In simple detail, the doctor explained how they would crack open my sternum and spread it apart to access my heart. This was way too scary for a twelve-year old to process but he said it would likely be down the line, when I was older.

I put it out of my mind until we got home. Usually, I had a five-minute phone time limit and could only make one call a day. But Dad told me I could talk all I wanted.

Uh-oh, I thought. *That's it. I'm dying.*

Oh, well. At least my heart condition got me out of P.E.

Two years after sliding a violin under my chin for the first time, I became the youngest member of the Des Moines Youth Symphony. The symphony was comprised of the best musicians in the city, brought together to form a full-size orchestra. And there I was, a sixth grader amongst high school kids, sitting in the back of the second violin section performing Beethoven's Fifth. Like many memories of youth, it was wonderful and frightening, both.

I was proud to be part of the symphony but battled the feeling that I wasn't good enough. Every practice, I lived in fear that they would discover I sucked and kick me out of the group.

My dad attended the all-parent orientation, asking about what periods of classical music we would be performing. He was as excited as I was scared, taking me to every practice and audition, talking about the details of the pieces we performed. I didn't see any other dads who were as involved as mine. My mother never came, but the older kids treated me well and some even took me under their wing. Youth Symphony became the heartbeat of my life, socially, musically—everything.

I loved the metallic cacophony of instruments clashing as we warmed-up, tuning and playing scales, goofing around. The good-natured competition between players, the way personalities fit by sections, the brass so brassy and the woodwinds seemingly so airy and light. And drummers, good Lord. So wiry and hyper all the time. These were my people. They understood me. Finally, I was among my own.

It felt like I was in way over my head, but I figured out how to fake it until I found my way. In symphony practice, "faking it" meant playing air violin when I got lost or couldn't follow the sheet music. I would pretend to be bowing and quietly play the notes I knew were right. But over time, with enough practice, I learned to pretend less and hit more of the right notes until eventually, I really was playing along.

Our Youth Symphony conductor was Dianne Pope. She was charismatic, well-dressed, and had the best thick blonde bob I'd ever seen. Dianne could be sweet and nurturing, but she demanded excellence and hard work. Ms. Pope didn't have children and was in the small minority as a woman orchestral conductor. When concert time came, she would deck out in full-on ball gowns or gorgeous tops with taffeta skirts. Ms. Pope's husband was some sort of local politician, but she didn't use his last name. I think she just wanted to keep her individuality.

I learned a lot about leadership from watching how Ms. Pope carried herself. If you can command the love and respect of a bunch of hormonal teens, you've got something special. Ms. Pope not only taught me to be a better musician, but she also helped me become a better person too.

In seventh grade, Ms. Pope arranged for me to audition for violin lessons from Dr. Wilfred Biel at Drake University, which was only about a mile from my house, so it was close enough to walk. Drake was an expensive private liberal arts college and people said if I was taking classes there, it must mean that I had talent, money or brains.

Unless there was some mistake...?

Even though it felt like I'd won the lottery, I was scared and questioning myself on a whole new level. I appreciated Ms. Pope's confidence but feared that Dr. Biel would be let down once he heard me play. After all, he was a college professor and I had just started junior high.

I started practicing up to six hours a day, sometimes skipping classes to prepare for lessons with Dr. Biel. There was serious pressure to be good, and he *always* expected me to play better than the week before. Biel was known to be a grouch who demanded perfection and though he never threatened to put me out, I felt the pressure to please him and didn't want to waste his time. I couldn't hide in the back of the violin section here. Dr. Biel was Concert Master of the Des Moines Symphony. Faking it would not do.

Despite his reputation, I suppose Dr. Biel saw my potential and how hard I was working to measure up because he kept on working with me week after week. Sometimes, when I played Bach's Air, he would slide his $38,000 Guarneri violin from the case and accompany me. To play with another musician, particularly a great one, is the best of feelings. There's an intimacy as the colors and lines intertwine, rising and falling, the whole far greater than the sum of its parts.

I didn't know all that when I was thirteen years old though. I just knew it was awesome.

After my lesson, Dr. Biel would walk me to the vending machine and let me pick out a treat. I remember staring up at the selections, torn between a Butterfinger's sweet, peanut-y crunch or the gooey caramel snap of a Twix. So many choices.

But I didn't want Dr. Biel to get mad and start scowling so I would usually just punch B6 for a pack of Nutty Buddys. They were my favorite anyway. Looking back, I think he knew I had it tough at home and it was just his way of showing me someone cared.

Working with Dr. Biel improved my skills, and I was promoted to first chair in the Callanan Junior High orchestra. But before long, I got demoted to the back of first section because I talked too much. Our conductor was a timpanist in the Des Moines Symphony, so I found it hard to give her much respect. Timpani wasn't even a real instrument. It was a drum! A drummer for a conductor? Please.

I was kind of a jerk to her. Remember being torn between snotty arrogance and raging insecurity? Yeah, well, then you remember junior high. Music was my whole life and like most teens, I thought I knew it all. As much as it sucked to get moved back, it made it easier to keep talking.

The house next door was nearly identical to our four-square-style home, except the layout was reversed so it was like a mirror image. The summer after seventh grade, a single mother moved in with her kids, Graham and Allie. Their mom, Martha, was a hippie-type who sat on their front porch playing the autoharp for hours at a time. I didn't know any Grateful Dead songs and Phish wasn't born yet, so, alas, we did not jam.

Allie was a year older than me, and her bedroom window faced mine. I thought maybe we'd have late-night talks across the distance, sharing secrets in the dark. But instead, I would sit in my room with the lights out, peeking through the curtain as she had big sleepovers with the other neighborhood girls.

God, I wished I could be over there with them, laughing and dancing to Rick Springfield, calling boys just to hang up, eating pepperoni pizza from Paul Revere's. But the twenty yards between our windows might as well have been Memphis to the moon. I would watch for a while, then let the curtain fall, pick up my violin and begin to play.

Her brother Graham was my age. He'd pack snowballs with ice and hurl them at my head, so I don't think he liked me too much, either. They were latch-key kids, coming home to an empty house, making their own dinner, doing whatever they wanted. Man, I was jealous of that.

Martha fell in love with the long-haired divorce attorney who lived up the block and eventually, they all moved in and rented their house out to a group of young men studying to be osteopathic doctors. I remember thinking that a group of young doctors next door could turn out to be be pretty cool.

One guy's name was Robert, and he had a reel-to-reel player and a ton of old jazz recordings. That was the first place I heard Monk and Mingus, Miles Davis's *Kind of Blue*. Robert played tenor sax, so we connected as musicians. He didn't really strike me as cute or handsome, but Robert was nice to me and soon enough, I conjured up something of a crush. He was a musician AND a doctor! Maybe, he could rescue me?

My new neighbors were sweet but never gave me much regard. They were busy med students, and I was just the awkward junior high kid next door.

The summer of '83 was a scorcher, and we were in the middle of remodeling our house. It was a full gut job, tearing out walls and ceilings, sawdust and drywall thick in the air.

We had a wirehaired fox terrier named McGuigan, but we called him Mac. Mac was not the family pet. He was my mom's dog. She doted over Mac, showering him with affection and praise.

Mac barked nonstop at the neighbor's dog and my mom would smack him with a rolled-up newspaper to get him to shut up. One day, Mac wouldn't quit yapping, so she hit him square on the back with her wooden Dr. Scholl's sandal.

Mac coiled back, whimpering in pain. It was just another frightening epiphany of how dangerous home could be. If my mother beat the hell out of her beloved dog, what would she do to me?

Our house was a wreck from construction, so my mom put Mac outside, even though it was over a hundred degrees. Robert noticed Mac laid out and panting in the sun. He grabbed one of the other med students and they ran over and tried to resuscitate him, but it was too late. Mac died of a heart attack that day.

I didn't see much of Robert or the other guys after that. I think they felt badly about Mac, and sorry for me and all the shit I had to put up with from my mom.

My brothers had been playing hockey since kindergarten. Jeremy was adorable in his little goalie gear but sometimes he would fall over and couldn't get up since he was basically one giant block of pads. Both brothers were as good at hockey as I was at playing the violin and soon, I found myself at the ice rink once or twice a week to watch their matches.

I liked running around the rink's bleachers, eating long ropes of red licorice. Now and then, I got to help out, taking money at the ticket window for open skating sessions. My mom even started working in the Ice Arena's concession stand. It was her first real job. She never graduated from high school.

My mother seemed to really enjoy working the snack bar. I was impressed that she was able to deal with customers and keep everything running smooth. I even got free nachos now and then.

With my mom's unpredictable temper, I thought she might throw a Coke in someone's face or kick a jar of jumbo pickles through the wall. But she didn't. In fact, the owners promoted her to the heated bar upstairs. And then, she became manager. We were the total rink family for a while, my dad cheering on my brothers during practice and games while I was running around sugar-rushed and helping out wherever I could.

The Des Moines Buccaneers were our semi-pro team, and we would all go to their home matches at the Ice Arena. Hockey nights were amazing, the goal horn blasting after a score, bone-rattling checks against the glass, fistfights and blood on the ice, stray pucks flying. More than once, I was nailed by a frozen, flying puck.

Thom Moreland was the Buccaneer's trainer. He was a big, brawny guy with kind eyes, always smiling and quick with a laugh. My dad liked him and I guess you could say they were friends.

At the time, I didn't understand why my mom was always at the rink, even when the boys weren't practicing, even when she wasn't scheduled to work.

Turns out my mom liked Thom too.

My parents let me attend a sleep-away music camp the summer after eighth grade. It was just down the street at Drake

University where I studied with Dr. Biel, but I was still thrilled to be away from home for a couple of weeks. Kids from all over Iowa came to play music together. I even got to stay in a college dorm.

It was mainly high schoolers at camp, and I quickly picked up a few new skills, like how to layer on shiny pearlescent lip gloss to look older than you really are. Also, summer camps have pools and if I planned on wearing a swimsuit in front of tons of other teens, I'd best get a razor.

"Razor?" I wondered. "For what?"

"Duh!" the blonde trombonist with sparkly braces said. "To shave your bikini line, of course."

No way I was shaving anything, especially down there. Nor would I be parading around a bunch of cute, horny boys in some neon green two-piece. I'd quit picking scabs and my skin had cleared up, but the thought of going underwater still freaked me out.

The music building at Drake had a long hall with rows of solitary practice rooms on each side. They were soundproofed but music still bled through the walls, and as you walked down the hall, random notes and scales would meld into a sort of shapeshifting, avant-garde fusion of free-form jazz.

Instead of scales, I would stand in my tiny practice space and coax the sweetest, most heartbreaking sounds possible from the strings of my violin. I may not have been the best technically, but I was broken inside and when the other musicians heard me pour out my pain, they would cry and beat on the door of my room, begging to come in.

Okay, that didn't happen. But I wanted it to, so bad.

Problem was, nearly *every*body at music camp was mega-talented. I remember one guy could play any song, in any key, no music needed. We would gather around the piano and sing Toto's "Africa" and "The One That You Love" by Air Supply.

You know those handful of times in life when you are exactly where you want to be, not dreaming about some perfect yesterday or abstract tomorrow yet to come? That's what that moment was for me. That's the power and the miracle of music, to lift you out of your circumstances and take you to a higher place, beyond age or race or religion or position or all that stupid stuff that keeps us so far apart. Music can break the hardest heart.

But I didn't know any of that then. I just knew that for one brief moment in time, I felt like the person I always wanted to be. I finally felt free.

I came home from camp and played violin for hours every day. I played with my windows wide open so everyone could hear. If someone could hear my heart, then they just might believe I was worth saving.

Little did I know, it would only put that much more distance between me and the rest of the world.

We got a new dog. A white English Bulldog named Maude. My dad would walk her after work.

Maude was a gift for my mom from Thom. Apparently, he liked her too. I wonder how my father felt walking a dog that my mom's boyfriend gave her. Did he know? Did they have some sort of arrangement? Was he simply dead inside by that point and just didn't care anymore?

I never asked.

CHAPTER THREE

RUN AWAY

"HOLD ON"

My high school life consisted of orchestra, Youth Symphony, and my church Matins choir. I also played in the pit orchestra for local musicals because the more I stayed busy, the less I had to be at home. I even started my own string quartet, one of the first gestures of independence not motivated by the fear of my mom. It wasn't that I felt unique or particularly gifted. I was simply always trying to prove myself.

There was a boy in our orchestra that I had a crush on. Sam was a cute smartass who could make his cello sing and as teenage hormones kicked in, I couldn't help but wonder what other magic his hands might be capable of.

Sam lived in a house across from the cemetery and his dad was a trombonist who bagged groceries at Dahl's. One weekend his parents went out of town and his big sister threw a party. When I arrived, everybody was drunk and dancing to the Moody Blues. (Stoners were too cool for image-driven MTV acts like Billy Idol and Duran Duran.)

Sam and I began a graceless sway to the music, staring deeply into each other's eyes. I followed him to his room, and we fell onto his bed. As we started making out, I felt his long, slim fingers slip beneath my shirt and bra.

This is it! This is what it feels like! I thought. *Thank you, God!*

We fumbled a little further as "Your Wildest Dreams" segued into "Comfortably Numb," putting the brakes on at second base. I returned to the living room and nursed a sloe gin fizz, feeling like maybe, I finally had a boyfriend.

The next Monday at school, we were tuning up in the band room and Sam told me that my legs looked fat, and my vibrato was too wide.

Oh, well. Whatever.

At one point during ninth grade, my grandma must have started making waves about my mom's behavior. This infuriated my mother, which made my dad's home life even more miserable than before.

Grams was forbidden to see or talk to me. But she was crafty. She showed up with her boyfriend Chuck to one of my concerts. "You *cannot* keep me from seeing my granddaughter perform," she announced to my dad.

I remember looking up from the pit during a performance of *Fiddler on the Roof* and wishing I could be up on stage, but the thought of singing and dancing and remembering lines— *in front of people*—was just too overwhelming at the time. So, I stayed hidden from sight down in the dark orchestra pit where I felt safe and knew my position.

My mom doubled down on me during freshman year, always yelling and screaming how stupid I was, grounding me, making me clean the kitchen and bathroom, then telling me what a terrible job I'd done. Around this time, my father decided to quit drinking. Sobriety is great but now he was gone to AA meetings every night and I was that much more alone. Secretly, I wished he were back in his chair, downing six packs of Bud. At least he'd be home.

But things were changing. I was coming of age and becoming a little more confident about my abilities. I'd started hanging out with the smart upperclassmen and looked to them for acceptance more than my family. They showed me that there was life outside of 29th Street and the more I got a taste of it, the less I could tolerate living at home.

So, I ran away.

I hid out at my friend Antoinette's house. She was senior class president, valedictorian that year. It wasn't like I was running with a troublemaker.

I waited an entire day before letting my family know where I'd gone. *That'll teach my mother*, I thought. My dad ended up letting me stay at Antoinette's for the whole week and when he picked me up to take me home, Uncle Kevin was driving.

By that point, I was ready to be some place familiar. At Antoinette's house, I couldn't help but feel like I was underfoot. Even if home sucks, it's still home. Maybe things would be different now that I'd taken a step to show my parents how I felt.

We drove straight down Kingman Boulevard, passing 29th. "Hey," I said, looking back at our street. "Where are we going?"

My dad turned and leaned over the back seat. "We're going to Broadlawns Hospital," he said, placing his hand on my knee. "To the psychiatric ward."

Emotions swirled. Fear, confusion, shame. Broadlawns was where poor people went. It's the place I was born. *Why would they take me there?*

When we arrived, my mother was sitting on a bench in the waiting room, glowing with hate, refusing to speak or make eye contact with me. A staff member came and led me to an office where a psychiatrist in a maroon sweater vest and bright yellow tie motioned for me to take a seat. He made small talk before asking the following questions:

Do you know what year it is?

Do you know who the president of the United States is?

Do you know why you're here?

I had no idea these were the standard "are you crazy" questions. I thought maybe the doc was off. The first two were easy.

1985. Ronald Reagan.

The third was harder. Yes, I ran away from home but admission to the psych ward seems like pretty harsh punishment for that? I told the psychiatrist about my living situation and my mom's abusive behavior, giving him a picture of my grim existence. After a while he brought me back out to the waiting room.

My parents had taken me to Broadlawns in hopes that the psychiatrist would commit me for at least two weeks. Instead, he told them, "Your daughter is in good mental health. We cannot admit her." Then he gestured to my mom. "However, I think she should go into therapy."

The look on my father's face said it all. My mother's fallout was nuclear, and it rained on him too. So, he sent me to stay with Uncle Kevin.

Uncle Kevin: Tall, gangly, super-smart. He drove a beat-up green Gremlin and had to stick his arm out the window to hold the door shut. Blasted Crosby, Stills and Nash on the Gremlin's 8-track. Worked for the local public television station. Not married. Uncle Kevin was cool, so I thought he was embarrassed by me. Or just didn't like me much.

It was awkward staying at Uncle Kevin's, so I slept on the couch and tried to stay out of his way. He didn't have a clue how to help a fourteen-year-old kid. I'd have rather stayed with Grams, but I guess Dad didn't want to start another war.

I just wanted to be back home in my own bed with my books, clothes, journals, and violin. Running away didn't accomplish much. I only wanted my mom to love me and see what my music teachers could see—that I was a good kid, talented and smart. Not perfect, but at least worthy of positive attention and love.

Back in the eighties, music and movies and television shows were hopeful and it made you think that people really could change, if you could just break through. I kept hoping that my mom would wake up, but she never did.

If anything, it felt like I'd only made things worse.

School was never easy for me. I struggled to concentrate on subjects other than music and art. Math was the worst. I could pull off music math, scales and time signatures, intervals, charts, rhythm and pitch—but traditional school math boggled my brain. Algebra was a required course, and it was like trying to teach cats to speak Japanese. I could not wrap my mind around abstract concepts such as $x^2 + y = z$.

In my case, $x + y = f$. As in *f*ail. So, I had to re-take algebra until I finally got a teacher named Mr. Brown. Though he was balding, his piercing blue eyes and sassy attitude intrigued me. This was back when a schoolgirl could have an innocent crush on a teacher, and it might even be a motivation to learn.

Mr. Brown explained algebra in a way that I could finally understand. I wasn't in any danger of getting a scholarship to MIT, but at least I passed. Algebra seemed pointless at the time but turns out those advanced math skills would come in handy down the road....

In sophomore year, Terry Branstad was elected to a second term as Governor of Iowa and my string quartet was chosen from players across the state to perform at his inauguration. Even if the gig only paid a hundred bucks, it was the first money I'd made playing violin. In my book, that meant I was a professional musician.

I was on my way.

I moved up to second chair in first violin section and joined my school's Concert Choir. I loved singing parts with other good singers but the thought of doing a solo still scared me to death.

Mr. Walag was our choir teacher, an electric little fellow packed with an infectious passion for music. He'd run up and down the rows, passing out sheet music, singing the various parts. There were never enough copies to go around, so we'd have to group up but sharing just made learning new pieces that much more fun.

About a month into the school year, Walag split us into quartets to practice auditioning for All-State Choir. There was a boy in my group named Phillip. He was a junior, a little reserved at first, but tall and dark, with an eager smile and *Risky Business* eyes.

Phillip was a classically-trained pianist and sang in the Matins Choir at Plymouth Church. Like me, he was a music nerd, and soon enough, we engaged in a gawky display of flirting, showing off, blushing, singing while stealing looks into each other's eyes.

One afternoon after practice, he shuffled around blankly, looking like he'd either eaten a bad Potato Olé or had something really important to say. I waited, watching his face. He smiled sweetly and took a deep breath.

"I thought maybe, uh . . . if you weren't already, y'know going with somebody else, you um, might want to—go to the Homecoming dance with me?"

My cheeks burned hot as excitement rose in my chest. I was too flustered to say anything at first. Finally, the reply came. "Yes!!!" I said, perhaps a little too enthusiastically. "I would LOVE to go to the dance with you!"

I floated to Jewelry Making class on a cloud. Then the question hit, the predicament every teenage girl faces after being asked to a dance. Especially one who has to scrounge outfits from the thrift store.

But what will I wear?

The answer? Grams.

In addition to author, speaker, fashion icon, and single mother of three who got her master's degree at age 40, my grandmother also knew her way around a sewing machine. She was as excited as I was at the news of Phillip's request. Grams got straight to work, making me a gorgeous formal gown, the top crushed black velvet with a subtle V-neck and puffy sleeves and a purple lamé taffeta bubble skirt to match.

All the other girls were buying their dresses from Gunne Sax or Laura Ashley but that was never an option for me. Still, I knew I would have something pretty to wear. And it would certainly be one of a kind.

My hair was barely shoulder-length, but I managed to corral it up into a French twist. Phillip had dinner reservations at a fancy supper club in the Ruan Building downtown where we planned to meet up with his best friend Miles and his date before the dance. Dining under crystal chandeliers while sitting high above the city was way out of my league, but fake it until you make it, right?

My biggest source of anxiety was the corsage. I had ordered a simple red rose boutonniere for Phillip, but would he know to get one for me as well? And do I put it on my wrist or is my date supposed to pin it on my dress? Do you know how awkward it is to have a boy fumbling and trying to safety-pin a flower to your chest while his dad snaps pictures and blinds you with the flash of his Polaroid OneStep?

Phillip's father was some big shot at the Polk County schoolboard and his mother a somewhat uptight stay-at-home mom. And by "somewhat" I mean like, totally screws-down WASP police. Mrs. Van Huesen was seriously miffed that Phillip had chosen to date a girl from the "wrong side of the tracks." Ugh. Like I didn't have enough mom problems in my life?

All her children attended Ivy League schools and as the last of four brothers to finish high school, Phillip was Providence-bound for Brown University as well. There was a lot of pressure placed on him to measure up, but he seemed to handle it all in stride.

Phillip was big into *Dungeons and Dragons*, loved Monty Python movies and had a Macintosh Classic, the first Apple product I had ever seen. It was a three-thousand-dollar computer the size of a suitcase with a tiny nine-inch monochrome screen. I used to doodle on the MacPaint app for hours and even though the best I could do were crude drawings, the Mac felt like space-age tech magically delivered straight from the Hand of God.

The Van Huesen's lived on 45th Street and Phillip would drive his mom's fire-engine-red Ford Sprint all the way down to 29th to pick me up for school. On Wednesday nights, we would drive to Matins Choir together for rehearsal. Our conductor took choir very seriously and if you missed more than three practices a semester, you were out. Phillip and I made the most of those three misses, roaming the little secret spots and back roads of town, windows down, wind in our hair, listening to the Violent Femmes sing about big hands and blisters in the sun.

Sometimes, he'd score the family van and we'd head over to the Raccoon Valley ball fields, long after dark, floodlights out, bleachers empty, and diamonds bare. Oh, to be young and free....

Actually, I think we missed more than three practices that fall.

That's okay. It was worth it.

CHAPTER FOUR

EMANCIPATION

"THINGS ARE BREAKIN' LIKE ROCKS"

The holiday season rolled around, and I had hopes to spend Christmas with Phillip. Then, Christmas morning, my mom pulled a butcher knife on me, the cops came, and my father stuck me in a shelter for troubled teens. I walked in with my clothes in a trash sack. The teens looked me up and down and laughed, calling me "preppy."

The shelter director stuck me in a tiny room with a dead-eyed blonde named Tracy. Her clothes were ragged, so in an attempt to make friends, I offered her the flannel blouse I got for Christmas. Then, I climbed in my bunk and cried myself to sleep.

When I woke up the next morning, the bed next to mine was empty and the curtain caught in the windowsill. My new roommate had taken the blouse and ran.

"Tracy's on drugs" an older kid explained. "Don't worry. She'll be back."

Drugs? What kinda place is this? I only knew about the homeless shelters and church soup kitchens where my friends would sometimes volunteer.

After a couple of days, I started to feel sick. I couldn't eat, my stomach hurt, and it felt like railroad spikes were being driven into my brain. "Can I have an aspirin?" I asked.

The counselor on duty handed me a tablet, along with a Dixie cup of water. "Take this right now, in front of me," she said. "I need to watch you swallow it."

That's strange, I thought. Evidently, some kids saved up their pills for an overdose attempt.

At some point, the other kids started to warm up to me. I wasn't as much of an outcast anymore. After all, I had been dumped in a shelter on Christmas night. Thank God, all my friends were off traveling with their families to places like Belize and Los Angeles where they'd get a deep tan to show off on the first day back at school. Even if they were home, I'd be mortified to explain my situation. But it didn't stop me from feeling completely abandoned. I had no idea how a shelter worked or what might happen to me while I was there.

The kids started talking to me, letting me sit with them at lunch and the TV room. They didn't call me "preppy" or make fun of me anymore. Maybe they thought I'm one of them.

Was I?

Many were homeless or poor or struggling with parents who were on drugs. But most of all of us were dealing with some form of abuse. It was a strange thing to bond over, but at least I wasn't the misfit anymore.

I spoke to my dad once a day, explaining that I was running out of clothes and needed to practice my violin piece for the upcoming concert. "I'm sick of this place," I complained to him. "When are you coming to take me home?"

My dad's replies were vague. "Let's not make any big decisions right now."

Maybe he didn't know what to do. My father coordinated the homeless projects for the city of Des Moines, but apparently, he wasn't ashamed of the fact that his daughter was staying at the shelter for teens. A few more days passed, and I was told there would be a family meeting with a counselor present.

"Tasha, your dad thinks it might be a good idea for you to go into foster care," the counselor said. "We'll discuss options at the meeting."

Foster care? Isn't that for little kids? I just wanted to go home. At that point, I didn't care if my mom was horrible to me, at least I knew what to expect. And why would my dad think foster care was a good idea?

The meeting was held on a Tuesday morning in the counselor's cramped, drab yellow office. The adults sat in a circle on student-sized chairs. I was in the circle too but felt invisible. They talked about me, but not to me. A social worker from foster care came down to explain how the process works.

"Your daughter could be placed at a home anywhere in Iowa," she told my dad. "It might be two hundred miles from

Des Moines. We won't know until we put her in the system and see who's willing to take her in."

"I'm in the ORCHESTRA!" I shouted, determined to make my presence known. "And I'm studying music with Dr. Biel, in like, a college-level class! I am NOT moving two hundred miles away! And there's NO WAY I'm going to be that far from Phillip!"

Seriously, what was wrong with those people? I could not believe my dad was choosing my mother over me.

Later, I asked to meet with the counselor one-on-one. A bookshelf sat across from her gray metal desk. I looked over the books. There were a few on child development, a set of encyclopedias, some law books. One of the other counselors pointed me to a thick volume on juvenile law.

I paged through it and found a part about "abandoned youth", reading as much of it as I could and trying to understand the legal jargon. Eventually, I realized that the system considered me an abandoned child, not a runaway, so I was free to leave the shelter at any time.

A glimmer of hope rose. *I can leave.* I called my father to tell him the news.

"Tash, I'm sorry," he said. "Your mother just isn't ready for you to come home."

I figured my mom was still mad about the police showing up at our house. My dad likely feared for my safety. I didn't know how my brothers felt, but the house was probably calmer now that I was gone.

"But, Dad, I don't have to stay here!" I replied. "And I am *not* going to a foster home! I'm calling Grandma."

One of the few things I could count on for breaks from the insanity of home were visits to my grandmother's house, the one on top of the big green hill. I dialed her number.

"Grams, I can get out of here! The counselors talked to a judge who told them about this loophole in the law! Can you come get me?" I begged.

"Tasha, there's too much ice on the roads for me to drive," she said, "You'll have to stay there until I can pick you up. Maybe tomorrow or the next day when the weather warms up."

Deflated, I called Phillip and asked him for a ride, but his mother wouldn't let him drive and this time, he did not defy her. Oh my God, if his mom thought I was trouble before, what would she think now that I was in the teen shelter? *Will I ever see him again?* I was questioning everything.

The ice melted and my grandmother came to pick me up. The ordeal had me too spooked to settle though and she seemed to resent having me around. Special occasions and infrequent sleepovers were one thing. I don't think Grams was ready to be a caretaker full time.

Pretty soon, my grandma had me functioning as her own personal cleaning lady, wiping her lipstick from the phone, keeping the shutters free from any speck of dust. She also began to confide in me in ways that weren't appropriate for a sixteen-year-old. One day, I overheard her berating her boyfriend. Grams was too polished to curse, but her tone and choice of words were so lethal that it was worse than profanity somehow. As it turned out, my grandmother was verbally abusive too. Crazy, but living at her house beat teen shelters or being chased with knives. At least for the moment.

Winter turned into spring. Phillip stuck with me through the worst. One day, he drove me to see my dad so I could make my case for moving back into the house.

My dad was working at his side job as a proofreader in a corporate office. We sat around a small conference table as I ran my fingers over the crusty scab I'd dug into my chest as if touching a worry doll for good luck. I told him that I wanted to come home. I preferred to return to the abuse of my mother—abuse I was at least familiar with - than the weird tension at Grandma's. But Dad said that it was up to my mom.

I called her from the rotary dial phone at Gram's. As the line rang, fear and shame tightened my throat. "Hello?" she answered.

But I was also desperate.

"Mom?" I began. "It's me. Can I come home?"

She paused. I paced and twisted the phone cord around my finger. "Oh, no, this isn't a good time," my mother finally replied, completely chipper, as if I were calling to schedule afternoon tea. "The house is a mess. Not until we can get it cleaned up."

She was so calm and pleasant, that it made me feel like the crazy one. *Hi honey, how are you? So sorry we don't want you here, but the house is just a mess. Gotta go! Have a great life.*

Besides, our house was always a mess, with newspapers, cigarette butts, album covers, and toys strewn through every room. I wasn't really shocked though. What did I think she would say? "Sure, come home so we can all live happily ever after."

I sat the receiver back in the cradle and stared at the wall. *Now what?* Only one thing seemed sure. At age sixteen, I was unofficially on my own.

Seriously? This is my life? How in the hell did things turn out like this?

I started combing the classified ads for a cheap place to live and trying to figure out my finances. I'd been working at a retirement home where I had to wear a hairnet and stiff white polyester dress. Kill me now, but it was a job. Then I got a position working nights and weekends at The Soda Jerk on 4th in West Des Moines.

The Soda Jerk was an old-timey soda fountain where I would shovel rock-hard ice cream into cones and scoop greasy ground meat onto white buns to make Sloppy Joes. We had a rainbow jukebox that played Sinatra and songs like "How Much is that Doggie in the Window." It was a popular spot for families and owned by a kind-hearted guy named Al.

Sometimes, Al would give me a lift after work, because otherwise, I had to beg a ride from co-workers or wait for Grams to pick me up. Minimum wage in Iowa was $3.35 and by the end of each shift I was covered in grease and melted ice cream.

I found a basement apartment in a brick building on Woodland Avenue, a two-bed, one-bath for only a hundred and thirty dollars a month. The morning I was planning to move, I sat Grandma down in the living room to tell her the news.

The sun was streaming through her big picture window. I fidgeted with my hands, suddenly forgetting all the things I had planned to say. Eventually, I spilled it out.

"Grams, I found an apartment," I told her, staring at a spot on the hardwood floor. "Phillip's coming later to help me move."

For hours she berated me, calling me ungrateful, saying she'd never be able to love anybody again. "How could you do this to me?" she cried.

I had never been so glad to see Phillip's van coming up that long, steep drive. We threw my few belongings into the back and left Grams standing in the doorway, still crying her eyes out.

Phillip helped me load my stuff into the new apartment and said he had to run to the store. I started unpacking, trying to arrange what little I owned in a way that didn't look like some lost kid playing house, wondering how in the hell I would make it on my own.

An hour passed. Phillip walked back in with two bags full of groceries and cleaning supplies. I looked at him holding those bags, so tall and dark and goofy and sweet. It was sad and somehow happy, hopeful and desolate and beautifully crazy all at the same time. It was a teenage girl having to move into a rundown basement apartment and a young, sweet boy, doing the best he could to help.

It was so many things that I am still trying to unpack that moment, even today.

CHAPTER FIVE

THE COURT AVENUE HUSTLE

"BLUE SKIES"

On the other hand, what teenager doesn't dream of having their own apartment? Excited? Yes! Terrified? YES. Excitedly terrified as I walked around my new space, flipping light switches on and off. Off and on. Nothing.

"Uh, Tash?" Phillip said. "You did call the electric company to connect your service, right?"

Oops. Faking it till I make it again. Good thing it was summer in Iowa because for a while, I didn't have heat or air. Or a TV. Or the deposit money needed to get my services turned on.

My dad was chipping in twenty-five bucks a month to help but that didn't go far. I'd have to come up with the rest somehow. Whatever I needed, whether it was food, approval, electricity, or love—I would have to figure out how to get it on my own. But change is a verb, they say. It's what you get up and do different the next day.

First on the list? Get a better paying job.

I applied at the Spaghetti Works downtown and got a call from the manager that same afternoon. "Can you start tomorrow?" he said.

"Are you kidding?" I replied. "I could start tonight."

Spaghetti Works was a fast-paced restaurant that served massive plates of all-you-can-eat pasta and the best cheese garlic bread on planet earth. I wanted to be a waitress for the tips but wasn't old enough to serve alcohol, so they stuck me in the hostess position up front "in the cage." I filled kids' balloons with a squeaky rush of helium from the tank, fending off bribes to seat the impatient. I ran my ass off doing whatever needed to be done to keep the spaghetti flowing and the customers happy and fed.

It was like a crash course in logistics, learning by doing, thrown in the deep end, sink or swim. Most days I was sinking, but then I realized a way to make it click in my brain. Being a hostess was a lot like conducting a symphony. You bring all the various parts together to make one sound, one movement, one song. When we're all in tune and on beat, everything flows. Once I realized I was the conductor, it all started making sense.

Everyone at Spaghetti Works was older than me but we all became friends and hung out together outside of work. One of the waitresses was twenty-six and we slightly resembled each other so she gave me her old ID. Now, I could sneak into bars. I could've cared less about getting wasted, I was just looking for a place to belong.

And besides liquor, what's in bars? Live music! We'd truck across the street after Spaghetti Works closed to Spanky's which featured live jazz on weekend nights. Susie Miget's group was the house band. Susie played upright bass and sang and if there was a cooler person in all of Des Moines, I could not imagine who that might be.

There I was, seventeen-years-old in a smoke-filled bar, sipping on cosmopolitans bought with a fake ID and watching Susie Miget sing "I Need an Umbrella to Protect Me From the Rain" I worked up the nerve to talk to Susie one night. Turns out she had studied with Dr. Biel too. That's when the lightning hit me. Ten years down the road, I would not be some waitress hauling mammoth plates of spaghetti to whiny kids.

In that moment, I knew exactly what I wanted to do.

It takes a lot of hustle to make ends meet so I started babysitting for a young couple to make extra cash. Janine (the mom) was nice, and her husband, Jeff, was funny and cute. They lived in the South of Grand neighborhood, home to the richest of the rich, massive houses with sprawling, manicured lawns. To live in South of Grand would be the dream life but it was so far out of my reach. Sometimes though, while babysitting, I would pretend it was mine, that I belonged there, with the elegant architecture and glowing blue pools.

Jeff would drive me home after babysitting, and that slim time together in the dark car was so thrilling to me. There was no flirting or anything inappropriate. It was harmless. I just liked the attention. Guess I was still a teenager in so many ways.

I didn't even have a license yet but was taking driver's ed. Janine still had her car from college and suggested she might be willing to give it to me, if I promised to take good care of it. (Uh, yeah!)

Sure enough, I inherited her dark brown Plymouth Valiant. Even though it was from the early 70s, that was my first car. Since I had no license, the Valiant stayed parked behind my apartment. After I completed driver's ed, the school gave me a slip that I could take to the DMV to exchange for my license. All I had to do was pay and get my picture taken.

But the fee was like fifty dollars and that was two weeks' worth of groceries for me. So, I decided the slip of paper was good enough and started to drive. I didn't even know you were supposed to have insurance.

Somehow, I managed to juggle schoolwork, Spaghetti Works, babysitting, and still have time to practice violin every day. But I was stretched thin and having a hard time making it to Youth Symphony and my other music requirements.

I'd stopped studying with Dr. Biel since the homeless shelter incident, but he agreed to let me come back. He was recovering from chemotherapy and seemed much different when I started again. I was used to his gruff demeanor but now he was gentle and soft-spoken, and looked like a frail, old man. I kinda liked it better when he was stern.

We met weekly and I paid the thirty-five dollar an hour charge for lessons myself. That was a lot of cash for a struggling teen, but it was already a big discount from his usual rate, and I appreciated him taking me back on. Dr. Biel wasn't as intimidating this time around but somehow, his newfound patience made me want to please him even more.

Months passed. I grew steadily, week in and out, listening to the old master's guidance. One afternoon, when our session was done, Dr. Biel stood and took a clear glass jar from the shelf. It was filled with folded bills.

"Tasha, this is the money you've been paying for lessons," he said, placing the jar into my hands. "Take it to Rieman Music. I've already picked out a bow."

I sat there, speechless, tears welling up. A good violin is crucial, yes. But most people don't realize the importance of a well-crafted bow.

I drove straight over to Rieman's. It was the very same place where my father bought my first violin. Four hundred dollars was far beyond our budget. I couldn't even think about money for a decent bow back then.

I carried the jar inside and placed it on the counter. The bow was waiting. I held it in my hands, tracing lightly from horsehair to tip, wrapping my fingers around the thin leather grip. Brazilwood, impeccably balanced, the frog of the bow neither too heavy nor too light. Smooth, supple, rich.

Perfect.

There was not enough money in the glass jar to cover a bow of this quality. I thought back to my first violin. *Would they let me make payments again?*

The man at the counter nodded to the jar. I slid it over to him. He nestled the bow into a velvet-lined case.

"Dr. Biel made arrangements," he said, handing me the case with a receipt on top.

Paid in full.

On the drive home, I held my hand out the window of the Valiant, catching air, thinking about Biel. About Janine and Phillip, and all the conductors and teachers and older kids who had taken me under their wing.

For years, I had been praying and waiting for someone to rescue me. But I didn't need to be rescued. I could rescue myself. What I needed, was to be loved, valued and respected. Which meant I would have to show love, value and respect to those who believed in me.

CHAPTER SIX

FULL RIDE

"PRISONER OF THE BLUES"

Phillip went off to Tufts University and fell in love with a girl from the dorms during a late-night game of Pictionary. Funny thing is, she played violin too. In my mind, she was so much better than me.

I was so sad but I guess I blamed myself. He was a good guy. Too good, maybe. It's hard to live with no regrets. In many ways, I am still hoping for someone as kind and good as Phillip.

I wasn't even sure if I would graduate high school, much less go to college. For senior year, I didn't even show up half the time and did the bare minimum required to pass. Who's got time for high school when you're on your own and working two jobs?

I'd turned eighteen and started to work as a waitress most nights. I also hustled gigs for my string quartet, playing weddings and receptions. High school felt like going backwards for me at that point.

Eventually, the school called and said if I missed any more days, I wouldn't graduate. This was February and I flew into a panic. How would I attend school daily for three straight months? Somehow, I figured it out, writing papers on restaurant tables between shifts, showing up to homeroom on three hours of sleep. Some of my friends took No Doze but with my heart condition, I was scared it might give me a heart attack so the closest I ever came to uppers or drugs was Mountain Dew.

May came and the school office said I could order my cap and gown. I sat in the auditorium not even sure the principal would call my name. Even if I did graduate, the guidance counselors at school indicated I shouldn't bother with college. I really did want to find a path up and out of my circumstances, but I didn't even know how or where to start.

But . . . my friend Michelle was applying to University of Kansas, so I did too. At least it was away from Iowa. What did I have to lose?

The application had an option to audition for a violin scholarship, so I checked the box and drove three hours south to show the committee what I had. I walked in, not really nervous, and had fun. I mean, sure, I played my heart out but that's the way I played every time I picked up the violin. Sometimes, in performing, you do better when the pressure's off. I walked out with a full ride to KU, so I packed it all up and moved to Kansas.

I figured out how to apply for financial aid and foolishly decided to live off-campus. Dorm life is fun, cheap, and the most socially abundant situation possible. Thousands of kids your age in a half-mile radius? But I'd already been living on my own for the past two years.

KU plugged me into their symphony and chamber orchestra, and I made a few friends before catastrophe struck in the form of mono. I don't know that mononucleosis would be considered a major tragedy by pandemic standards, but back then, it devastated me.

I got so sick, that I had to drop out and move back to Des Moines, convalescing on a futon mattress on the floor of my father's rundown apartment. He had just started divorce proceedings with my mom. Somehow, she got custody of my brothers, so Dad holed up in a crusty, one-bedroom apartment out in Sherman Hill. He did fix-up work in exchange for rent, kind of like Mr. Miyagi without the karate and sage insights.

To his credit, Dad made it as nice as he could for me. When my brothers did visit, we all slept on the couch and floor. It was almost like old times, minus the wrath of mom.

I couldn't work and my dad didn't have any extra cash to spare so I lived off my student loans. Months passed before I got well. I didn't go back to KU. Classes were boring and my grades sucked. I didn't want to go to school. The only thing I cared about was music. Music and cute, quirky boys.

I started dating a violinist who had already graduated from Iowa State. (After the mono cleared up, of course) Sonny was an introvert who drove a black Chevy Impala with a red Batman logo painted on the door, which in 1989 was a magnet for weird, artsy girls like me. He was witty and brilliant with the communication skills of a drunken aardvark.

Unfortunately, Sonny was also mostly drinking when I saw him. He'd say he was coming over at eight and show up around midnight, with a six-pack of Milwaukee's Best, the name of which was either some sick Wisconsin joke, or a sad commentary on quality control from our neighbors in Milwaukee. Regardless, our dates pretty much revolved around Sonny's consistent consumption of beer. This got old quickly.

I asked him to meet me earlier, to go on regular dates and stop drinking so much, to be more dependable—in short doing the one thing you should never do in a relationship, trying to get the other person to change. Just that quick, Sonny was gone.

Tired of laying around depressed all the time, I transferred to Iowa State. I needed a goal, something future-minded. It's not that I was so enamored by the idea of college, but in the late 80s, higher education was everything. Especially if you wanted to feel like you were trying but had no idea of what to do. If you were clueless, college was a good place to hang while you tried to figure it out.

Like sports, proficiency in music can open a lot of college doors. I drove up to Ames, auditioned and received a full scholarship. Financial aid once again enabled me to move into a tiny apartment with Valerie, my best friend from high school. Student loans, Pell grants, Federal loans. The money was out there if you knew how to jump through the hoops. I had no money management skills though and was always broke.

Sometimes I'd wait until the landlord knocked on the door before paying rent. Valerie was older and more responsible. I think she realized I didn't have anyone to teach me those things so even though we were both barely getting by, she helped me out, showing me how to buy groceries and save, teaching me to cook on a budget. Most importantly, she listened to me ramble as we both shared all our crazy college dreams about what we would be someday.

Valerie was in school studying art, but I wanted to sing. I loved the emotion, the ability to make people feel the way you want them to feel, to laugh or cry or miss some old lost love. I liked being on stage. Not hidden behind a music stand in a crowd of violinists either.

Secretly, I dreamed of Broadway. The only thing that stood in my way was the ability to act, dance and not completely freak out about performing in front of a crowd. Also, I still was scared I'd forget the lyrics.

Academically, I didn't do much better at Iowa State. Biology, American Lit, Psychology—all that stuff was so dull to me. Music was the only place I wanted to be. I played in Iowa State's Symphony and early into my first semester, our concertmaster had to leave. The professors thought it would be a good idea for me to replace him. *Me?*

I went straight home and cried. Good tears. Panic mixed with joy. It was a high honor with a lot of high pressure too. The concertmaster is like the conductor's first lieutenant. After the audience is seated, the concertmaster comes out to tune the orchestra to A440. It's all very formal.

I dreamed of Broadway and was a "conductor" of sorts for an entire Spaghetti Works restaurant, but the pomp and circumstance of the concertmaster role was something I just wasn't ready for at the time. Still, I was on scholarship and the university needed someone to step up. I didn't feel like I had a choice. Sometimes opportunity can feel like a jail sentence, but the discipline was probably good for me. I was so consumed by music that I didn't have the time or interest to drink, do drugs, or sleep around.

I still went to bars though, mostly holding a bottle and taking slow sips, faking drinking to meet people and be around friends. I saw my old high school guidance counselor in a bar called The Duck Blind one night and he said, "I thought you'd end up in a gutter, dead. Glad to see you made it."

Made it? I guess I was faking that too.

Part of my studies at Iowa State consisted of playing in a string quartet. We were an oddball mix of personalities with nothing in common except a love for classical music. Even though the quartet was not meant to perform professionally, I believed that we could make money on the side.

What college kid doesn't need extra cash? I certainly did. Hunger stirs vision. I saw opportunities to make income from everything I was good at. Or even *close* to good at. Was it a natural tendency towards entrepreneurship or a by-product of living in survival mode?

Maybe both?

I designed a business card but couldn't figure out how to transfer the hand-drawn violin for print, so I dipped into my student loan money to have it professionally typeset. Whatever it takes. I would've gone into debt to market us as a string group for hire. Back then, a business card was where you began.

As soon as I had a thousand cards, I started to promote my group whenever and wherever I could. The "Sapphire String Quartet" started out playing small ceremonies and gatherings around campus and when we landed a gig for author Jane Smiley's Pulitzer Prize reception, I thought we'd finally hit it big. For "Canon in D," a couple of Vivaldi's "Four Seasons" and some background "Air on the G String," I went home with a cool fifty bucks. At least I didn't have to eat Top Ramen that week.

One night I was at a Pearl Jam / Red Hot Chili Peppers show with a friend from school named Jill. We met some guys and they invited us to an afterparty at the Holiday Inn. Jill and I were jumping on the bed when a guy with long blond hair walked in.

The jumping stopped. Jill was a cute and perky cheerleader. I grabbed her elbow and leaned in close. "Do not even *think* about flirting with him," I whispered. "He's mine!"

He noticed me noticing him and introduced himself. Soon enough, I was pretending to be drunk as we danced to Anthony Kiedis sing about lust in a phone booth and shining his lady's diamond. Hey, it was the 90s.

Anyway, the guy's name was Nick and as the only not-really-drunk person at the party, I ended up driving him home in his gold Porsche 911. "Um, what do you do?" I asked Nick.

"I'm an architect!" he slurred.

We went back to his place and engaged in some sloppy making out but that's as far as I let it go. I slept on his couch instead. The next morning, he woke up, kissed me on the forehead and said, "Thanks for getting me home, Natalie."

Not a good start.

Turns out Nick was nine years older and working at a firm back in Des Moines. Despite our introduction, he could come off as affectionate and mature, responsible even. I liked him and we soon became a couple.

Christmas rolled around and I was excited to finally spend the holidays with my new, handsome, older man. But then he stood me up, calling the next day to say, "Sorry, I got really drunk and like, *super*-high."

I started realizing Nick wasn't exactly the person I had hoped or imagined him to be. Nick wasn't even the person that *he* was hoping to be. I wasn't some doe-eyed virgin, but at heart, I was a nice Midwestern girl who'd been through some hard times and wanted better. And sometimes, when we want better, we compromise. We see things for what we want them to be rather than for what they really are. It's not like I had many examples of healthy relationships to draw from.

So, even though my instincts told me to run, I stayed. I needed someone to take care of me, to pay attention to me. Someone to love me. Someone, anyone, was better than no one.

At least that's what I believed at the time.

Time passed and things calmed down. Then, I didn't hear from Nick for a few days. I panicked until he finally called to let me know me that he'd wrapped his precious Porsche around a freeway pole while driving drunk. He was pretty upset about the car. Drinking and driving should've been a giant, flapping red flag, but truth is, bad as it sounds—nearly everybody did it back then.

Nick got a little cottage on a long street lined with trees and when summer break rolled around, he asked me to move in. My mom had a new husband—remember Thom from the ice rink? Yep. I borrowed his truck to haul my stuff over to Nick's.

Oh, yes, my mother. Where has she been? Well, for the most part, still crazy and mean as hell. But now and then our paths crossed when I would visit my brothers. She tried to be decent, sometimes. When I was sick with mono, she brought me some yogurt-covered pretzels. But it never lasted long.

Moving is always harder and takes longer than you think, and I was late getting back with Thom's truck. My mom called.

"Quit lying to Thom, you fucking little bitch!" she ripped. "Don't think I won't shoot your stupid ass. I'm looking at my loaded .308 right now!"

My mother had taken up deer hunting with Thom. She had a rifle. For all I knew, she had it cocked and loaded and was on the way. I always figured someday she'd lose it and really do something dangerous. Nick's backdoor faced the woods. I could imagine her out there, watching me through the crosshairs.

I called Thom at work. It had a been a long time since I'd had a run-in with my mom, but all those old awful feelings came rushing back. "Thom, my mom threatened to shoot me," I said. "Please lock up the guns."

Thom agreed. He loved my sad old, broken, bat-shit crazy mother. But Thom knew she was horrible to me.

It's not like I had my life together. Soon after moving in, I discovered that a drinking problem wasn't Nick's only demon. There were other addictions, problem behaviors he was struggling with as well. I responded by downing codeine cough syrup and crying myself to sleep.

Finally, I got up the nerve to see a therapist and spilled my story out. She listened patiently before gesturing for me to stop. "I'm sorry," the therapist explained. "But I just don't know how to handle this kind of case. I'll need to call my supervisor in."

Well, that was mortifying. My problem was so sick and twisted that even someone who hears problems for a living couldn't handle it.

Nick wasn't a bad guy. He was just trying to outrun his past and reach for something higher, but deep-seated issues kept dragging him down. In some ways, we were a lot alike.

I left Iowa State and tried to start over once again by transferring to Drake University where I had studied as a teenager and gone to camp. Dr. Biel had since passed away, and Grams was now an adjunct English professor. I knew my violin would once again grease any sticky wheels and land me a scholarship. Sure enough, they offered me a full ride. I studied under a new violin professor, but he was flirty and inappropriate, and it just made me miss Dr. Biel.

Wanting to stretch out, I had started playing guitar more and trying to write songs. I signed up for private voice lessons but my instructors at Drake blocked me from taking the class. I didn't understand the role of university politics at that point. The music department wanted to keep my focus on violin.

I *really* wanted to sing, so I secretly withdrew from all orchestra and violin classes. If they weren't going to let me sing, then I wasn't going to be their pet violinist. Passive-aggressive? We didn't even know that word back then. I was "sticking it to the man." Felt good too. I liked the power. Even if it meant losing my scholarship, I liked doing things my own way.

Drake was the first place I had access to technology, so I began sneaking into their computer lab to teach myself word processing and rudimentary graphic design. I needed money so I set up to showcase at a local bridal fair to drum up business for the Sapphire String Quartet. I kept the name from the group at Iowa State, assembling a new set of players from Drake.

Using my newfound design skills, I made a banner with a picture of me playing violin and wearing classy diamond earrings. Okay, *faux* diamond but they were still expensive, so I returned them to the store soon as the photos were done.

The bridal fair went well, and I ended up with tons of bookings. So many engagements, that I had to hire Drake music professors and Des Moines Symphony musicians to fill in with my quartet to meet the demand.

I don't think they liked being one-upped by a young, female student.

CHAPTER SEVEN

EXIT, WEST

"CAN'T WE FEEL"

My wedding business was booming as I had tons of friends and contacts around the marrying age. I started doing solo wedding gigs too, singing and playing the violin, performing the deep alto version of "Ava Maria" or "All I Ask of You" from Phantom of the Opera. Wearing a vintage black sheath dress with white polka dots with matching pointed-toe pumps, I had a Jackie O vibe and enjoyed the attention and praise, helping people feel good on their wedding day.

Nick and I were doing okay, making the relationship work, battling our hang-ups and age difference, even going to Sunday services together at Plymouth Church and participating in their music programs. One night, we were out to dinner, and he started talking about going to San Francisco to study architecture at Berkeley. At first, I thought he might be dumping me but then he turned and said, "So, how would you feel about moving to San Francisco?"

The Golden Gate Bridge seemed a million miles from Iowa, but cold, hard winters were wearing me out and I was ready for a town with more culture and better opportunities. My dream was New York City, but California sounded good. It wasn't like I was going to graduate from Drake. Besides, why did I need a degree in music when I was making good money playing in a string quartet? I was hiring professors with PhDs to work part-time for me! That was the value of a music degree. I could always go back to school in San Francisco.

"Sure, let's go," I told Nick. "But long as we're leaving, we ought to have a big party so our friends can say goodbye. Maybe our minister will even give us a blessing."

"If the minister is going to bless us, why not just get married?" Nick said.

"Wait," I said. "What?" I sat there, stunned, staring at my pasta salad. "You seriously want to get married?"

We scheduled a simple ceremony for three months later. My dad and Nick's parents split the cost, since most of it was DIY. Even though I despised my mother, I still felt like I should let her know.

We hadn't spoken since the incident with Thom's truck, but Valerie told me she was working for a local caterer, so I made an appointment for a tasting. I wanted to shock, surprise and maybe even embarrass my mom. Her own daughter coming in for a tasting for a wedding that she didn't even know about. And she'd have to "serve" me as a client. We would never have been able to afford hiring a caterer, but I wanted her to know about my wedding. And to punish her, I guess too.

When we arrived, my mother wasn't there, so I sent her a nice letter instead. She called shortly after, excited, acting as if she hadn't recently threatened to shoot me with a deer rifle, suggesting I register for Calphalon cookware.

Nick and I were set to get married in the park at Saylorville Lake. The night before, I had serious cold feet, but it was too late. Dad had already spent fifteen hundred dollars. I couldn't let him down.

The morning of my wedding was sunny and clear, so I took that as a positive sign. But by afternoon, a storm blew in and I had to wait under a bus stop before starting my bridal march. Uncle Kevin came with a golf umbrella to walk me down to my father who was decked out in a coat and tie.

As the harpist played "Rhosymedre" by Ralph Vaugh Williams from the shelter of the park's pavilion, I walked stiffly with a frozen smile, already running possibilities for annulment or divorce. Fake smile. Fake marriage. *When will I ever make it and stop having to fake it so much?*

My mom was there, behaving. My brothers too. It was all a blur.

Soon enough, the minister asked if I took this man in sickness, health, for better, worse, and all the whatnot that goes with marriage vows. Thunder crashed and the rain pounded harder. I nodded blankly and repeated the words, "I do."

Do I?

Afterwards, Nick and I ate barbeque, cut our little homemade wedding cake and slow danced to Whitney Houston's "I Will Always Love You." Des Moines flooded (it was the great flood of '93) and depression set in. We did not leave right away for California.

Nick and I fought all the time. I cried a lot, and hated being a "wife," but we kept trudging on. The apartment in Sherman Hills was too expensive so we moved into a rental house behind my dad's. So much for the gold Porsche lifestyle.

By this point, my brothers lived with my dad and had moved away from sports and started to play guitar. Sometimes, in the evenings after work, my father would fire up the big Weber charcoal grill and we'd all play music together. Even if married life sucked, it was nice to be back together with my dad and brothers again.

I was folding shirts at Eddie Bauer for five bucks an hour, working temp jobs through ManPower, and booking as many wedding gigs as possible, hoping to put back enough money so we could move. Maybe a new start in a new city would help?

I saved up four thousand dollars and we finally made the jump, renting a Penske truck to move. I bawled through six states, from Midwest to Pacific Ocean, all the way to our new room in a two-bed apartment in North Beach. That's right, *room*. Six hundred dollars a month just to rent out a bedroom in someone else's apartment. That's how much our big, beautiful place back home in the Sherman Hill neighborhood had cost.

After a massive time-signature fail (I was playing 2x faster than what the others were playing) while playing for hire with a string quartet in Nob Hill, I formed my own group once again. I was a much better employer than employee. Besides, while I was able to transfer to a Bay Area Eddie Bauer store, time was passing, the bills were piling up and Nick was still unable to find a job.

When times are tight, you have to get creative. Fortunately, a new technology had come along that held great promise.

I could not have dreamed of the internet when I was a teen. None of us 80s kids could. A wireless pocket phone that offers millions of songs, movies, photos, books, and a worldwide connection to your friends? Not even in science fiction.

I quickly became addicted to tech and the opportunities it could provide. Even though we were broke, I understood the principle that opportunity requires investment and in 1993 I took out a loan to buy a Macintosh Quadra 650. It was the Tesla of computers back then, the fastest, most technologically advanced machine on the market. It was also the most financially advanced, costing nearly as much as my car and so big and heavy that users dubbed it the "Fridge."

The Quadra was the ticket to catapult my art, music, and dreams into the future. Through the magic of dial-up internet, I could now get on this exciting new frontier known as the World Wide Web. America Online ruled in that day, sending out promo floppy disks offering free trials and local number access at blazing speeds so you too could experience the thrill of having the AOL guy announce, *You've Got Mail!*

Insert the "OK Boomer" joke of your choice here, but I am telling you—you have no idea of the wide-eyed joy one felt upon hearing Mr. AOL's chipper baritone informing you that someone out there in the cyberspace—in a time when people still hand-wrote letters and sent them cross-country with a stamp—had sent you an email.

That dream you hear when people wish they could go back in time and snap up the domain rights to Target.com, or Sears.com and Beatles.com? I used to surf the net before the big companies had websites. I had the idea to buy up domain names but never followed up on it. Besides, I was struggling to pay the note on a three-thousand-dollar Mac.

Back in that era, I was a lettering artist, doing calligraphy for wedding invitations and advertising agencies. I wanted to turn my personal lettering style into a digital font. San Francisco / Silicon Valley was the right place to be, but I still didn't have access to the knowledge on how to get it done. I have a lot more dreams than I have the time and the means to get done, and difficult as it might be to believe, it really did seem impossible to contact someone or find help back in that day. We were still searching through the phone book for information.

This was a time before spam, viruses, or phishing schemes. I'm sure some naughty pioneer had internet porn out there somewhere, but it certainly wasn't anything you'd stumble over while innocently searching for ping-pong paddles or cat toys. I would explore cyberspace for hours on end. AOL's new music portal had me the most excited. I was ecstatic over the notion that I could upload my demo songs onto a website where people could listen from around the world.

That was a staggering thought. In that day, there was no distribution. The only way to hear a new artist was through radio or live shows. You could burn a CD or copy a cassette but that was it. There was no real way to get your music out there to the people.

Until the internet! Back then, we connected over the phone line with a modem, which made a screechy noise that sounded like my computer was screaming robot profanity at another computer until they allowed us entry to the information superhighway.

Once connected, I could upload a song. This incredible feat of technology took about an hour. One song—one hour. Unless someone called me. The incoming call would boot me off AOL and I'd have to make the robots scream at each other again and start all over from scratch. A little blue upload bar would crawl across the computer screen to let me know the progress, marking the percent completed one number at a time. Even if I didn't get a call, sometimes the network would drop at 86% loaded and I'd have to start all over again.

After somewhere between fourteen and thirty-six hours, I got three of my songs loaded and was one of the first artists on AOL! Worldwide access! Anyone with the internet could click a button and hear my songs. In 1993, that was hard to fathom.

Creating a website for my string quartet was next on the list of things to check out. I was still advertising in bridal magazines but could grasp the importance of a website as a marketing tool. The *HTML for Dummies* book helped me figure out the basics and before long, my investment in a Mac was starting to pay dividends.

Small ones, sure. But it was worth it to be on the cutting edge.

CHAPTER EIGHT

WELCOME, OLD SOUL

"OVER THE MOON"

A friend from back home came up one day and we took a road trip to Sterling Vineyards in the Napa Valley, riding the gondola to the top of Diamond Mountain to sample their various wines. I looked out over the rolling hills and lush, green countryside thinking that life in San Francisco just might work for me. A change of scenery really does help. Or maybe it was just the wine.

Nick pressed for intimacy once we were back in our room. We weren't having sex anymore. Never did much. I gave in, it was sweet, and before long, I found myself married and pregnant.

Nick continued combing the Yellow Pages and cold-calling architect firms for a job while I worried that we'd have to move back to Des Moines. I was hustling and in addition to weddings, started playing coffee shops and house concerts with my guitar, writing songs, trying to pour out my feelings through chords and lyrics.

Can't we feel the magic we used to feel?
Going back just a few years?
We laughed and we played
every moment we were happy...

I called my dad to let him know he was going to be a grandfather. I was twenty-three and halfway across the country, far from friends and family, feeling alone. I'm sure my father was trying to soothe my fears, but his reply came as a shock. "Well, when your mom was pregnant with you, no one even knew it."

What-the-*fuck*? What kind of parents hide having a brand-new baby girl? Grams didn't even know she was a grandmother until I was nine months old! Is that why my mother called me a bastard? I had a ton of questions but didn't get many answers from my dad and it wasn't like I was going to ask my mom to tell me what was going on.

After nearly two months in California, Nick landed a job with an architecture firm, and we moved to Alameda. I took a job at a pre-press shop across the street from Nick's office and was thrilled to have insurance and benefits. My new employers were supportive when it was time to have my baby and I fully intended to return six weeks later.

But then baby Bennett was born. I looked into her eyes, fell in love, and had an epiphany. Why would I hand my child over to a stranger for ten hours a day if I had another choice? I was pretty good at freelancing. I could play music and start doing graphic design. I could work from home and raise my new baby girl.

Being a mom turned my world upside down. All the love I never got from my own mother came flooding into my life in a different form. I was able to be the sort of mother that I had always longed for. Finally, I could give and receive unconditional love. It was a miracle. Still is.

Nick finally had a job, and I was playing music and doing graphic design in one of America's coolest, most creative towns. We had a precious baby girl. Despite these things, marriage started to feel more like a cage than a dream. Before Bennett's second birthday I asked for a divorce.

With time, I started to feel more confident and less trapped by the mindset that I needed someone to save me. I knew that I could not only take care of myself, but my baby too. Knowing that didn't make it any less scary though. There was some peace in knowing that Nick and I really did try our best.

I took a job at Shugart Matson ad agency. Even though I wanted to stay home with Bennett, I really needed the money and had a starting salary of $37K which, as they said in 1997, was serious dough. Shugart made me traffic manager for all their projects, which meant I had to know the status on over two hundred jobs every day.

Computers were slow-moving behemoths in that day so I would haul around large envelopes with each job inside. It was mass chaos. I was always in the weeds. But by this point I was all-pro at faking my way through. I had no experience being a traffic manager at a giant firm. But I'd been a hostess at a busy restaurant and concertmaster for a hundred-piece orchestra. I knew how to multi-task. If you hang in long enough, you figure out the secret: everybody's faking it to some degree.

A few months in, Shugart gave me a raise. I was still doing string quartet gigs for cocktail parties and wedding ceremonies while singing with my jazz ensemble for receptions. I'd perform for a wedding on Friday night and have shows all day Saturday.

Once, I did four back-to-back. I booked the events, lugged the fifty-pound JBL speakers, set up mics and music stands, and ran the mixing board before changing into a dress and high heels to sing. I was exhausted and loved it. Made good money too. Nick had been paying me alimony, but he was living in an economy apartment, so I told him to stop. He continued to pay child support and that was enough.

Frederica Von Stade, the famous opera singer, was hosting a fundraiser at her home and I was asked to sing. Guitar case in hand, I arrived at exactly the kind of stunning mansion you'd expect a sophisticated opera star to live in and started having second thoughts. I had confidence in my voice, but if I really wanted to impress? Violin. *Should I run home and get my violin?*

Too late, I'd already been spotted. They welcomed me inside. The room was jam-packed. I set up in the corner and begin to sing, a few Shawn Colvin covers and an original or two. I was only there for background music, a local artist doing the non-profit thing.

Frederica called the room to attention. I strummed softly, waiting to hear what she had to say. "Everyone please welcome this wonderful young vocalist who just moved here to Alameda. She is such a beautiful songbird."

Did another young singer walk in? I turned to check and make sure. Nope. Frederica Von Stade, the famous singer, was telling everybody to be quiet and listen to me. It was one of those moments where you feel excited and mortified at the same time. But I knew how to perform. I knew how to play. If you can wrap your head around it, pressure is a performer's best friend.

Everyone got quiet as I began to sing. Von Stade's eyes were upon me. Charm, beauty. Made her debut with the Metropolitan Opera at just twenty-five. Intimidating? To say the least.

I pressed on, pouring my heart out best I could until the song was over. Then, I started looking for an escape. Frederica approached and threw her arms around me.

"Oh, my God," she gushed. "You have the most beautiful voice!"

"Really?" I replied. "Thank you, Mrs. Von Stade. So much."

"Oh, honey," she said, laughing, "Call me Flicka. Please!"

I thanked her again and put my guitar in the case. Flicka stood beside her baby grand and begin to sing. Her tone was so amazing I nearly fell to the marble floor. Beauty, charm, God-given talent—and grace. Flicka was kind. My voice could not compare to hers. Not even close.

Nick brought Bennett by after the event. Flicka had a beautiful Victorian dollhouse and Bennett was smitten, opening all the little doors and windows, crying with outstretched arms when I tried to pry her away.

A few days later, Flicka showed up at our apartment and gave the dollhouse to my daughter. I stood there, awestruck and on the verge of tears, thinking back to my own little tin dollhouse, how my mother had trashed it in a rage. "Oh, gosh, Flicka," I said. "You shouldn't have."

"Like I need a dollhouse," Flicka replied, waving me off like it was no big deal. "Let Bennett have fun with it for a while."

I wasn't looking for a mother-figure, but as Flicka bounced Bennett on her hip, singing and blowing air-kisses, making my baby laugh—I thought it sure would be nice to have the love and support of someone like her around.

Flicka was a fervent philanthropist and started asking me to play at the many charity events she held. I performed with Phil Lesh from the Grateful Dead, legendary jazz mandolinist, David Grisman. Like Flicka, they were all cool, down to earth people. Flicka and I even started doing shows on our own to support music education in schools.

Flicka's encouragement made me want to focus more on music so I left Shugart and started looking for a part-time job that would enable me to spend more time performing. Roger Becker of Becker Media hired me to work Tuesday through Thursday from ten a.m. to four.

My job title was "media buyer" but there were only two of us, so I jumped in and did everything that needed to be done. What I lacked in experience, I made up for in curiosity and persistence, teaching myself better web design and Photoshop so I could build Becker's website and create print ads in addition to selling our services. Sometimes, I was even able to write, perform and produce jingles for our client's ads.

Roger was relentless, so I was too. Within a few weeks, he started calling me "Pitbull."

You learn something everywhere you go. Every person and each position has something to teach you about life. Even if it's singing a perky radio jingle for Cash One PayDay Loans. I don't know where or how I got that attitude, but it served me well. It helped me rise above my circumstances and my upbringing.

A four-day weekend gave me time to pursue my musical dreams. I had been performing since seventh grade. Now, I wanted to become a recording artist.

I began writing songs like crazy, weekends and squeezing in time after work, always bent over my guitar or piano, pouring my heart out in melodies and words. I was boy/man/relationship crazy and expressed all my dreams and despair through song.

I'd been performing live with top-notch musicians. Aretha Franklin's drummer, Jon Evans, bassist for Tori Amos, others that had experience touring with big names. Most people don't realize that you can be wailing on stage for thousands of people but once the tour is over, you're playing birthday parties and Bat Mitzvahs to pick up extra cash.

I should've mentioned that I highly encouraged both my brothers to move out to the Bay Area with me so they too could escape our broken family and have a better start. They'd long since hung up their hockey gear and were nearly as deep into music as me. Justin played electric bass and Jeremy had become a seriously gifted guitarist. We almost had a family band just amongst ourselves.

When Jon Evans opened his own recording studio, I decided it was time to record my first CD. Back in the nineties, every musician hoped and prayed to be signed to a major label deal. That's how you knew that you had made it. I didn't have the time or patience to play that game, so I started my own label, Poignant Records. By then, I'd figured out that I function better calling all the shots.

I was excited, nervous and scared (common feelings for me) about making a record with big league players. They were studio pros with big names on their resume. I marveled at the seemingly endless numbers of cords snaking from the soundboard into mixers and amps, the towering racks of effects with banks of switches, knobs and sliders to adjust. Sitting quietly to the side, I watched everything, taking notes of the lingo, hungry to learn.

We did most of the takes together as a band, separated by sound barriers and isolation booths. Several cuts featured Justin on bass and Jeremy laid down some tasteful guitar parts. If any of my tracks sounded great, it was because of the group effort to color and shade the melodies and lyrics I had brought in. Once we'd finished a good run-through of the song, we would go back and "punch in" to fix a mistake or take another run at a passage.

Then, I would go into the booth to record my final vocals. Usually, I'd make three or four passes on the song and work with the engineer to splice together my best performance.

We kept the first pass for "My Sleep." We were just practicing, but the engineer hit "record" and captured our performance. It wasn't perfect but the emotion was right. (They tell me that's how books work too.)

"Her Life" was the name of my first record. I wrote every song, played several instruments, and sent the CD around to as many radio stations as I could. Female singer/songwriters like Sarah McLachlan and Natalie Merchant were hot in that era, so I knew I had a good shot of getting some airplay, especially regionally.

Being a part-time musician was not enough. I wanted more. But I was also twenty-nine years old and making six figures at Becker Media. I wrestled that decision back and forth, but in the end, I knew I had to give all my attention to music if I were to truly live with no regrets.

CHAPTER NINE

ALL IN

"UNCHAIN MY HEART"

After "Her Life" was released, I started to gig at venues that supported singer/songwriters. I even got invited to play the infamous San Francisco bar and laundromat Brain Wash, and The Red Devil Lounge. I was learning a lot about becoming a professional recording artist by pouring over magazines like Acoustic Guitar, JazzIz and going to conferences like ROCKRGIRL as well as playing showcases. Most of these shows were done for no pay. I knew experience was the most important compensation and that doing it over and over would prepare me for bigger stages.

The Lilith Fair festival had sparked an entire new slew of female talent as well as a focus on female musicians and I wanted a piece of it. I was armed with just enough information to get ahead, studying books like Donald Passman's *All You Need to Know about the Music Business* from cover to cover, learning about copywriting, songwriting ownership, publishing rights, contracts, and typical record label deals.

Another book talked about doing a series of living room concerts to promote your performing career. This was intriguing to me. My daughter, Bennett, was young and I couldn't travel cross-country sleeping on couches. But I could create a concert series in my own town of Alameda.

I named the series *First Saturdays in Alameda* and scheduled the shows with a quirky opener such as punk rock accordion player Duckmandu, followed by a local up-and-coming artist and closing the night, a headline act. Flicka even came out to perform, bringing the house down with a set of Broadway numbers.

There are always things you can't prepare for. Like the singer who dropped way too many F-bombs for a family audience. Parents were glaring at me, kids in tow. So, I sent him a note saying *can you cut the cursing, please?*

A portion of every ticket sale went to the Alameda Education Foundation to support music in public schools. Churches and clubs donated space and a dedicated group of volunteers helped set up chairs and work the snack bar. We wanted to sell wine but that required a special permit, so we provided a "free glass" with donation to circumvent the local laws.

I was hands-on with every aspect, from running cables and mixing the sound to designing posters and putting up flyers all over town. The music program at my school was a lifesaver and I've heard similar testimonies from many misfit kids. When I believe in something, I am ruthlessly tenacious.

First Saturdays in Alameda was a success. Hundreds showed up for the concerts on the first Saturday of every month, and I was able to pay the musicians, make money, and donate to our public schools.

I didn't want anyone to think I was creating a platform just to promote myself, so I was careful to only perform every three months or so. It worked and I was able to gain a loyal following without having to leave Bennett and travel from venue to venue across the country.

The artists loved it because they had an attentive audience and could sell their CDs and other merchandise. The audience loved it because it gave them something fun to do with their families and a place to discover new music. I loved it because I had created something special and was learning new things about the music business from bottom to top.

I had a growing kid, and couldn't shirk too much stable income, so I started my own business to book shows for myself and other artists, calling it Entire Productions. I knew I'd have to sacrifice some comforts to give my company a fighting chance, so we moved from our three-bedroom Craftsman to a small garden apartment. Bennett and I slept in the same room.

I had thought up the name for the business back while pregnant with Bennett. My friend Stacy and I were pitching to a merchant banking company called ChinaVest in hopes of landing the contract to create their website and translate it into Mandarin and Cantonese. Stacy was a graphic designer/rocker girl from N.Y.C. who greeted me every morning by asking to rub my belly and say "hi" to baby Bennett, and her husband, Eugene, was developing the NetDoubler application for Apple computers. I was doing graphic design on the side and had just enough courage and marketing savvy to believe we could pull it off, so we called our new company "Entire Productions."

Did we understand web design and coding well enough to complete the task? Not really. Did we speak Mandarin or Cantonese or know anything at all about private equity banking? Not a clue. But ChinaVest took the meeting with us and that gave us hope. And if we got the job, we figured Eugene could help us out with the tech stuff.

We did not get the job.

I decided to recycle the name for my new entertainment production company, and clients thought Entire Productions meant that I would handle the *entire production*. I can't say that belief was a bad thing. Entire was run completely out of my apartment and I soon began thinking of ways to expand.

Once Bennett started Kindergarten, I became friends with Kappi, a mom in our parent group. Kappi ran her own event company called Grace Under Pressure Productions and offered me a desk in her office at a very reasonable price. She even hooked me up with my first big client, Oakland City Center. (Which I still have twenty-one years later.)

I knew I would need help, so I tested the waters with interns first before bringing someone in part-time. Then, after a few years of hiring contractors, I hired my first full-time employee,

Catherine. She was an everything girl (meaning she could do everything) so that was awesome. Even though Catherine was versatile, I was still clinging to the belief that I had to be in control of everything or else my clients wouldn't be satisfied.

Example: Around this same time, a woman called wanting to do a backyard barbecue with music.

"Okay, what would best set the mood for your party?" I asked

"I want a salsa band," she replied.

"Does the band need to be Cuban natives?" I said. "Do you want people to dance?"

San Francisco is very diverse. We have hundreds of salsa bands. I know the genres, the lingo, how music can make or break any party. The customer doesn't always know how to explain what they want, and I felt like if I didn't ask the right questions, we might end up disappointing our clients. Above-and-beyond excellence is important to me. Therefore, I believed that I had to have my hand in every detail.

I discovered this is all too common with entrepreneurs. Even with help, the owner becomes convinced their business will fail unless they do it all. Often, businesses fail *because* the owner tries to do too much. So, even though I had help, I wasn't letting Catherine truly help me.

Shortly after, Kappi asked me to help her get two hundred invitations out to people all over the country, hand-delivered *in person*. Not just major cities but small towns as well. She wanted it to be like a Publisher's Clearing House experience, surprise knock on the door, gold foil envelope, balloons.

Creativity wasn't the problem. It was a matter of logistics. I was tempted to take it all on myself, but I remembered my days in the restaurant business, seeing the owner or manager try to be head chef, front of house, hostess, janitor, cashier—it never worked. I thought back to management jobs where I had to take on too much. It's an ego boost and you may burn bright for a moment, but eventually, you will burn out, limited by your own abilities. You will never grow your business past yourself.

So, I bit my tongue and let Catherine take on Kappi's entire project. I hadn't heard people encouraging me to delegate at this point, but I had an inkling that for Entire Productions to grow, I couldn't be the one doing all of the things. Catherine dove in and figured it all out, local balloon vendors, confetti, partnering with FedEx to not only get the invitations out and into people's hands, but also making it a one-of-a-kind experience.

I realize it doesn't always go that smoothly at first, but the experience opened my eyes. Catherine had ideas that would've never crossed my mind. She had fresh angles, experience, and skills to draw on that I did not possess.

A lifetime of sugar rush and the avoidance of exercise drove me towards the gym where we had a circuit training teacher named Greg Matthews. The other moms in my class drooled over Greg but they were all married and enthusiastically encouraged me to go out with him.

Greg was a triathlete, so I hired him to teach Bennett to swim. She was four at the time and screamed so loudly that I jumped into the pool in my workout bra-top and bike shorts.

Very embarrassing. But also, clumsy and cute enough to get the attention of our Adonis-like trainer? Somehow, it was.

"I hate swimming pools," I confessed, as water ran from my nose.

"You can swim though," Greg said. "Right?"

And that's how I started taking swim lessons, at the same time as Bennett. Greg even taught me to put my head underwater without losing my mind. For all that motivational life motto talk about "jumping in the deep end" it was nice to be able to do it and not get triggered by some cruel flashback from kindergarten.

After we had been dating and moved in together, Greg helped with the metaphorical depths too. He noticed my mood swings and depressive fugues, how they'd strike out of the blue. Instead of criticizing or pulling away, Greg listened, asking the right questions, encouraging me to seek professional help from a psychologist he knew named Lilly.

Dr. Lilly was a brassy gal from Boston who also worked out at our gym. The thought of telling my deepest secrets to a stranger was terrifying, but since I'd seen her fully naked and pregnant in the locker room, I figured we were kind of on even terms.

After a while, she suggested that I may benefit from an anti-depressant. I always thought those were for other people, but the idea gave me a giddy sort of hope, so I immediately made an appointment to see a psychiatrist and picked up a prescription for Zoloft.

It worked! Not perfectly. Not overnight. But the moods were not so dark and the darkness not so deep. I still felt sadness and anxiety and sometimes even overwhelmed. But I could function without crashing and for me, that was a miracle. Enough of one to make room for a second miracle, and soon Greg and I were pregnant.

After doing enough gigs at cafes and clubs, I discovered that the money was in jazz and started a second record, called *Talk to Me Nice*. KCSM in San Mateo agreed to play tracks and invited me on for an interview. The next night, my phone rang.

"Natasha Miller?" the man on the line asked. "This is Bobby Sharp. I just heard you on KCSM. Your voice is beautiful."

"Oh, um. Okay, thanks."

"I'm a songwriter and I'd love to send you some of my songs, if that's okay."

"Yeah, sure," I said, not knowing what to expect.

"You might know one of the songs I wrote," Sharp said.

Probably not, I thought.

With great pride and enunciation, he continued. "Unchain my Heart," he said.

"The old Ray Charles tune?"

Who didn't know that song? Uh-oh. What had I gotten myself into? I didn't sing like Ray Charles or Joe Cocker who'd had a hit with the song in more recent years.

A few days later, I received a package with a lead sheet, handwritten note, and cassette tape of Bobby playing piano and singing his song, "My Magic Tower." Though it was a demo, the performance was riveting. I knew I had to record this song.

I called Bobby back and asked him to meet me at a coffee shop in Alameda, close to where he lived. He hesitated, saying he didn't get out much anymore but finally agreed. An old red Cadillac rolled up and parked at the curb of the coffee shop. Bobby stepped out, stooped and skinny, wearing a loose-fitting faded blue jacket and jeans.

We spent a couple of hours talking about life and music. After forty years in the music business, Bobby had given up trying to get his songs published and had become a drug counselor until his retirement in 1989. Since then, he'd spent his days visiting the homeless in West Oakland, helping friends and neighbors or even strangers he read about in the paper. He didn't say any of this in a bragging way, just matter of fact. At age seventy-nine, Bobby preferred a quiet life.

He talked about growing up in Harlem, how his father had been a concert tenor. Bobby didn't get any formal training until after he returned from World War II. Then, he got his heart broke and spent twelve hours a day at the piano writing songs.

Sarah Vaughan cut one of his songs and he penned the title cut, "Blues for Mister Charlie," for the James Baldwin play of the same name. Around this time, he got addicted to heroin and wrote "Unchain My Heart" so he could score enough money for his next fix. He wrote the song in one night, and the next day took it to a publisher who bought it for fifty bucks. Ray Charles recorded the song in 1961 and it became an instant smash. Two years later, Bobby sold his share of the song for drug money.

"So, what about you," Sharp asked. "What's your story?"

I told him about growing up in Des Moines and being on my own at sixteen, violin scholarships and string quartets, getting married in a monsoon, and when I said that lightning striking during your vows should've been a sign from God, Bobby laughed, but *with* me, not at me, like he'd made enough mistakes in life to understand. I talked about my divorce and trying to raise a daughter alone, torn between music and the stability of a job with benefits, how security can often be the enemy of dreams.

I don't know why I opened up so much, but this sweet old jazz crooner seemed like he'd heard a lot of stories in his time. When I was talking, he didn't look away like most people do or try to offer advice. He just listened.

After coffee, he showed me more songs, each one seemingly better than the last, a treasure trove of uncut diamonds. Music can make strangers instant kin and as we said our goodbyes, I knew something special had taken place.

"I'm going to record your songs," I told him. "I have to."

Bobby nodded, smiled, and said that would be nice. Then he eased behind the wheel of that long red Cadillac and slowly drove away.

CHAPTER TEN

DEBUTS

"MY SLEEP"

At nine months pregnant I made my debut with the Oakland East Bay Symphony. With a crowd of two thousand before me, the orchestra began the haunting introduction to "My Sleep," a song I had written. Hand on my swollen belly, I began to sing.

> *You came to me in a dream last night /*
> *How lovely it was...*

I wasn't debuting as a violinist but as a vocalist. The entire orchestra was playing a song that *I* wrote. I was shaking and not in the best voice but loved that I was performing this piece with my unborn baby inside. I could imagine telling him about the performance when he was older, showing photos from that night, pushing the hair back from his sweet face while singing the song acapella for him.

As we went into the chorus, my baby kicked, and I knew he could feel the music all around us. I caught his tiny foot and massaged it back to rest.

At thirty-seven weeks pregnant I began to feel contractions and reported to the hospital. The maternity nurse called my OB/GYN. She was told to give me a shot of morphine and send me home.

I turned down the shot and returned home without seeing a doctor. Why would they offer morphine to a woman over nine months pregnant? I was so sick and miserable that I sent eight-year-old Bennett to stay with a friend. The sickness lingered for two excruciating days and at one point, I became so weak that I had to roll off the couch and drag myself to the bathroom. I couldn't eat and was dying of thirst, drinking gallon after gallon of water with no relief.

Monday came and I crawled to the car and somehow made it to my doctor's office on autopilot. She passed a sonogram over my stomach, and I waited for her report. The silence shot a wave of fear through me. "You can't find a heartbeat?" I asked in the frailest voice.

"You need to get to the hospital," my doctor said. "Can you get yourself there, or should I drive you?"

The hospital I was supposed to go to was thirty minutes away but there was an emergency room just steps from her office. I was delirious from pain and confusion, so I didn't ask why.

I waited in the doctor's office for Greg to pick me up as she passed me in the hallway on the way to see other patients. We sped over in his pickup, every bump twisting my tortured body with pain. Sheer grit carried me into the hospital and up to the maternity floor. I whispered my name to the clerk and passed out onto the gurney.

A nurse pulled me out of my clothes and into a hospital gown, hooking me to a bank of monitors. Beeps, blips, it was all like a dream, fading in and out, voices in the room. A tall Indian doctor entered and examined me. "No heartbeat," he said, in a soft and lilting tone, almost musical. "So sorry, no heartbeat. So sorry."

I faded away again, stirring to hear one nurse ask another, "Fourteen vials of blood, are you sure?"

When I woke again, Jeremy was standing at the foot of my bed. *If my brother is here, it must be bad.* I turned and threw up a thick oily, black substance. Jeremy held his phone to my ear.

"I'm sorry," my mother's voice said. "I love you, Tasha…"

I opened my mouth to reply but nothing came out. If my mom's calling with those words, I must be dying for sure.

The information came in pieces. *Protein in her urine . . . blood pressure 135 over 110 . . . liver failure . . . kidney failure . . .*

The brain shuts down with major organ failure. You can't make basic decisions, like calling 911, or demanding to go to the emergency room twenty feet from your gynecologist's office door.

"But what about my baby?" I asked.

The hospital gave me a strong dose of magnesium to prevent a stroke and Pitocin to induce labor. I lay for hours, waiting to give birth. Early in the morning of March 4th, Aidan was born, weighing eight pounds, five ounces, and twenty-one inches long.

Although his lips were a cold shade of blue and his skin jaundiced, Aidan was absolutely beautiful. He had a full head of brown curly hair and the tiniest, elegant fingers. I held him briefly before falling back to sleep.

For the next twenty-four hours we all held baby Aidan. Greg and his parents, Bennett, and my dad. Then, they took my sweet baby away.

My health got worse. I was visited by a revolving door of grief counselors and doctors of every discipline: nephrologists, perinatologists, hematologists, and occasionally my OB/GYN.

I felt nothing. No pain, no fear, no sadness. I could not eat. I could not cry. I could barely speak and was only able to sip from a straw held to my lips. Family and friends filtered in and out of the room. My dad stood guard to make sure no one lingered too long. Flicka brought me a boombox and a stack of CDs.

Nurses drew blood every four hours, to the point where they had to start looking to my feet for usable veins. One doctor mentioned dialysis, talking about it as if I wasn't even in the room.

"She is not going on dialysis," my dad insisted. "We're going to figure this out." He knew I was unable to advocate for myself and began asking more pointed questions, pushing back, making sure I was a priority and not just rolling over to the best guesses and whims of the medical staff.

At some point, I decided I needed to try to get up and walk. My friend Rebecca was there, and she helped me sit up and swing my legs over the side of the bed, holding my catheter bag so it wouldn't get tangled in my feet. Crisis reveals who your real friends are.

I tried to stand but my legs were spaghetti, crumpling under the slightest weight. Rebecca plopped me in a wheelchair and took me for a spin around the hospital anyway.

After a week, it was time to be discharged. The ride home was surreal. Everything felt dangerous, traffic zooming around me, tall buildings looming, ready to crush my bones to dust, everything a threat in my most weak and vulnerable state.

Greg helped me into my apartment. We were never married, nor did we live together at this point. But a new kind of romance began to take shape, sweeter, deeper and more meaningful than before. Going through disaster either pulls you apart or pushes you together. Thank God, Greg pressed in, becoming my protector. Even though our baby was stillborn, he was still a father. The grief was massive, but we would find a way forward together.

I wasn't capable of caring for Bennett yet, so my dad stayed to help. She was having a hard time coping, trying to wrap her young mind around all that had happened. Every night she would wail, and I would pull her close against me until we both found some level of comfort and peace. I was still afraid that death could strike at any moment. In that beautiful space between awake and asleep, I would jolt upright, gasping for breath, fearful and unsure of whether I was drifting off to sleep or dying.

My father wanted to pursue a lawsuit against my OB/GYN for negligence. She knew about the protein in my labs, the high blood pressure, signs that something was terribly wrong. Lawyers warned that even if we did "win," we could only expect a thirty-thousand-dollar settlement at best. We learned that was the maximum value of a baby that died before birth. Had he taken one breath outside of my womb it would have been a much different story.

To me, that would only add suffering to tragedy, so we let it go. The doctor knew what she did. She would have to live with that knowledge for the rest of her life.

Aidan's bassinet was still set up next to my bed. I would open my dresser drawer and look through his clothes, Pooh Bear onesies and tiny shirts with rainbows and balloons on the front. I knew I should be grieving, crying, screaming, kicking that dresser through the wall. I hurt for my dad. I hurt for Bennett. But as for my own loss, I could not feel a thing.

Greg visited every day and a nurse acquaintance stopped in to check my vital signs. When Greg mentioned holding a funeral for Aidan, I just pushed him away. Even though he found a burial plot and chose a casket, I refused to set a date. Finally, a mutual acquaintance named Liz walked in, sat before me and in a tone both loving and stern said, "Natasha, it's time. We are having Aidan's funeral on March 17th." When you are shell-shocked and dead inside, sometimes you need someone to take control.

On the day before the funeral, Greg told me he was going to the morgue to see Aidan. I couldn't even fathom such a thing. Bennett caught wind of his plan and demanded to go. She wanted to see Aidan's toes and read *Guess How Much I Love You* and *Goodnight, Moon* to him.

There was no way I could go through with that. But Bennett made me. Somehow, even at her young age, she understood that in order to heal and move on, we have to say goodbye.

The morgue was dark and cold. Aidan's body was displayed inside his tiny casket along with blankets from his baby shower, little stuffed lions and giraffes, notes from family and friends. Bennett reached into the casket, picked Aidan up and carried him over to me.

I sat there, cradling him in my arms, staring at his beautiful face. I did not know what to expect other than the worst, thinking that my baby would be frozen or stiff with rigor mortis. But he was not frozen. Only cool, blue and so very peaceful.

Bennett unbuttoned the legs of the onesie and pulled out his teeny foot, her fingers holding his toes. We took turns holding him, reading the words.

> I love you high as I can reach
> across the river, and over the hills

For the first time, I was able to cry.

Aidan's funeral reception was held on the waterfront at Bay Farm Island on St. Patrick's Day. A bagpiper played "Amazing

Grace" and over a hundred people showed up to help us say goodbye. A priest from the Episcopal Church performed the service. I sent word that I was burying my child and didn't want to hear anything about God or Jesus, but he read from the Bible anyway. That really pissed me off.

I told Bennett we could leave without watching the casket being lowered into the ground. She stiffened up. "No, mama," she said sternly. "I need to bury my brother. I have to see the casket go down."

After the funeral, my dad had to return home. Before he left, he sat at my piano and played "Somewhere Over the Rainbow," a song we used to sing together when I was a kid. I tried to sing along but my voice was weak and cracking. It felt like music was over for me. I could not imagine standing on stage, smiling in the face of what had happened. It didn't feel like I could ever be happy again.

Greg stopped by the next day. "We're going to the pool," he announced. "Get on your water shoes. You're going to walk with me."

I still felt like a zombie but went through the motions since I was too exhausted to object. The water felt good, swirling around me. Moving felt good. Feeling good felt good.

Greg got me swimming again after that. Swimming, focusing on breath and form, all the metaphors of water and baptism and resurrection. I don't know if Greg thought of any of it that way, but he knew I had to get moving.

"You know what, Tash?" he said one day. "You should come with me to masters."

Masters was a practice group of hardcore swimmers made up of mostly previous swim stars in high school and college. They did two-a-days, practicing in the pool at six a.m. and again at five in the evening. Greg was the fastest swimmer in the masters' group—the one to beat, and the nicest of them all.

"I'm the antithesis of you," I told him. "I can't even finish one lap. How can I be in the masters?"

"Just come with me," he said. "You'll be fine."

We went three or four times a week and even though I was weak, everyone encouraged me and welcomed me in. I needed community and over time, I got stronger and faster.

After one morning swim, Greg announced, "Hey, I signed you up for the city meet."

"Oh, hell no," I replied. "You've lost your mind. I'm just now getting to where I don't freak out sticking my head under. There's no way I can dive off the edge into four feet of water."

Greg was unfazed. "You can do it," he said, grinning. "Watch and see."

There I was, at the City Swim Meet in Alameda, California, me—the shy, snot-nosed, kid from Iowa who couldn't even go underwater. Wearing a swimsuit in public, no less. Life is so insane.

The pistol sounded. I sucked up courage and swam my best breaststroke and a beautiful but sluggish freestyle. I did not win. I did not swim fast. But one year after my son's death, I dove in and swam with all my heart.

Victory is not the most important thing. It's the struggle and fight, the lessons we take from our scars. It's getting back up when life has kicked the absolute shit out of you, and you cannot find a way to go on.

But somehow, you do. Somehow, you learn to live again. Through love, support, friendship, laughter and reaching down to help someone else along.

That's a key part, helping others. I knew what I had to do. Make good on my promise to Bobby Sharp.

CHAPTER ELEVEN

CREATE YOUR OWN STAGE

"MY MAGIC TOWER"

I transposed Bobby's song, "My Magic Tower" into my key so I could try to sing it. Like the best of torch songs, it was sad and sparse with just a flicker of hope. I stood at the piano, eyes closed, singing of spiraling magic towers and the power of make believe.

They say music soothes the savage beast and the beast in me was grief. In my darkest moments, the song had stayed with me, drawing me in, a shelter from the storms around. It brought me back to the magical towers I had built as a child to lift me above my troubles, a safe place to hide until the storm passed by.

It would take a lot of work to get back to a place where I could sing in public, but Bobby's songs deserved a new audience and I wanted to surprise him by performing "My Magic Tower" and "Unchain My Heart" in concert. No one had paid attention to his music for a long time, and I was on a mission to change that. I needed a mission, something to reach for, a reason to get up and push.

Working out in the pool had strengthened my lungs and after a few false starts, I found a sweet spot in the song. *I can do this*, I thought. *I'm far from top voice but at least I can still sing.*

I called up Bobby and invited him to First Saturdays in Alameda, the concert series I had created. We'd kept in contact, and he knew what I had been through, the fear that I may never return to the stage. I started in on "My Magic Tower" and looked out beyond the lights, finding Bobby in the crowd, tears in his eyes and a broad smile spread across his slim face.

That was all it took for me to catch the music bug again. Bobby Sharp had an entire catalog of classics and I started toying with the notion of recording an album of his originals. Bobby had given me the lead sheets and demos, so I got to work transposing the cuts into keys that suited my range. After we'd made some leeway, I let him know about my plan.

"Hold up," he said. "I don't want you paying for everything. Need some money for the studio? I could give you a few bucks…."

I didn't understand why this was an issue. Bobby lived in a modest bungalow with every surface coated in a film from cigarette smoke. His kitchen was bare, and he wore the same outfit most every day, short-sleeve plaid button-down, usually blue, baggy Levi's, toes poking out of the end of his shoes. If he were offering to foot the bill, I sure didn't see any sign of money.

He was driving us to the recording studio in Berkley when he handed me a check for twenty-five hundred dollars. "No, no, no," I told him, pushing the money back. "This is what I do. You're not paying for this."

Bobby smiled, still holding out the check. "Let me tell you a story...," he said.

Seven years after selling his rights, Bobby learned he'd been cheated out of royalties. He sued and the court restored all his rights. At a clean and sober fifty-one years old, Bobby Sharp became a multimillionaire.

Money doesn't mean that much later in life. By then you're used to living a certain way. So, Bobby liked to give his money away. He'd drive down to the homeless camps in Oakland—tents sporadically coupled under the overpass—and hand it out two dollars at a time.

We worked out a deal and *I Had A Feelin': The Bobby Sharp Songbook* was released on my label, Poignant Records. Rave reviews ran in newspapers like *The New York Times*, *San Francisco Chronicle*, and *Wall Street Journal*. Bobby had been out of the music business for over forty years, and he finally had a record out. A lot of papers told the background to our project as well. It was quite a story. We had both been through a lot.

With that, I was back into music and back on stage, even singing the National Anthem for the Oakland A's in front of forty thousand fans. Baseball fans, not jazz. So, I sang it Americana style.

Bobby drove me over to Oakland Coliseum. People wonder what it's like to sing "The Star Spangled Banner" in a giant stadium. It's truly an honor, and honestly, for a singer, it can also suck. Baseball parks do not have sound systems conducive to an acapella version of an incredibly difficult song. Slap back, reverb, treble-rich echo bouncing off plastic seats.

I'd sing "Oh, say, can you see?" and a second or two later, hear my voice starting the line again. That'll wreck singing in time *or* in tune. Did I mention no monitors? But a pro rises above, so I stuck my finger in my ear, tapped my foot to stay in time and soldiered on.

My cousin Joshua was in the Marines, so I thought about his service and sacrifice and sang the song for him. But it was not fun. Still, once I got to the *la-hand of the freeee*. . . the entire stadium stood and erupted as I waved from the Jumbotron. Okay, that part was fun.

After that, I got calls to sing the anthem at many other pro sporting events. I sang it again for the A's several times and eventually, they got in-ear monitors which made the song a much better ride. I performed "God Bless America" at a Raiders vs. Broncos game, "O Canada" for the A's again and multiple renditions of "Star Spangled Banner" for events from basketball games for the Golden State Warriors to The America's Cup sailing competition.

I always took the anthem seriously. Those words carried serious weight. I knew I needed to be excellent, but not perfect. Perfection is sterile. It's not human. It's not emotional. Excellence is something we all can do.

My cell phone rang, and I checked the screen. It was my friend, Kappi.

"I scored two tickets to the Grammys," she said. "Can you go?"

"What?! Wow!" I spit out the words in disbelief. Grammy tickets were impossible to come by. "How did you even . . . YES! Yes, I will go with you!"

Bobby insisted on buying me a black taffeta dress from Ann Taylor for the ceremonies. I think it was on sale for $100. It was too long so I had it hemmed but then it was too short, so I concentrated hard on keeping my knees together and tried not to flash Sting. We snagged a limo ride from the Biltmore to Staples Center, and somehow security waved us through, and we got to walk the red carpet with the celebrities. (Except the carpet was green because Heineken was sponsoring the Grammys that year.)

We paraded down the press gauntlet, flashbulbs popping, reporters yelling for Heidi Klum and Fergie, Gwen Stefani and her posse of Harajuku girls. Nobody screamed for us or took pictures, but I still felt like a princess that night.

Our seats were in the upper balcony where we were surrounded by record company executives and artists whose moments had passed or not quite arrived. From our high position, I could see the massive amounts of colored tape marking the stage, the moving of the sets, all the complicated behind-the-scenes mechanics necessary to put on such a show. I watched each detail, dreaming about someday walking the carpet as a Grammy nominee, being called to the podium by Clive Davis to accept the award for Best Jazz Vocal.

Once the ceremonies were over, Kappi and I attended CBS's two-million-dollar afterparty with catering by Wolfgang Puck and a performance from Earth, Wind & Fire. After that night, I joined NARAS (National Association of Recording Arts and Sciences) so I was officially a member and eligible to attend the Grammys. With my record releases, I was also able to cast votes for the award process.

The next time, I took Bennett along. We put on fancy red dresses and watched as the celebrities arrived, then we headed straight for the McDonalds concession stand. Bennett was a cute kid, so she was able to snag plenty of autographs that night.

Stevie Wonder closed the show, and I was surprised to see most of the audience leave while he was still playing. Seemed crazy to me, but these people had wardrobe changes and fabulous parties to attend. I still fantasized about being called to the podium but as time passed, I learned that things are not always as they seem. Not even the Grammys. If anything, it made it easier for me to sing and play simply for the joy of performing.

Sometimes Bobby would duet with me at concerts and despite being an eighty-year-old chain smoker, his voice was still silk. He could hold a note so long, riding the current up and over the changes. After all those years out of the business, he still had it. And even after going through hell, I still had it too. I'd set out to help Bobby, but truth is, he helped me too. We helped each other find a second chance at music and life.

My publicist, Marshall, capitalized on our story and it was picked up across the country. The *Los Angeles Times* ran a piece about our music and friendship that had various production companies vying for our life rights. The Bobby and Natasha story still hasn't made it to film, but we had a lot of fun conversations with Hollywood producers.

"You can't dance on every stage," Bobby would tell me, usually when I was multi-tasking too much. He taught me the importance of pace, not to rush, to let the story have its way. He found happiness in the small things, going to McDonald's for coffee and a hot apple pie, driving down by the bay, bonfire smoke and seaborne fog, the smell of cable car brakes and salt water in the air. Bobby loved buying scratchers from the California Lottery to hand out to friends or strangers even, just for that one quick burst of joy.

He couldn't believe I didn't have cable TV, so he'd go down to the Comcast office and pay for my service directly so I couldn't turn it down. He bought tons of books for Bennett to read and even plotted with my friends to surprise me with a Toyota RAV4.

I was getting booked solid at great venues, and Marshall got me a gig at Yoshi's, which is like the Carnegie Hall of jazz in my opinion. Before the show, my dad stuck his head backstage. "Tash, you did it," he said. "The ticket line is all the way around the block!"

After selling out Yoshi's, I was in high demand and got a slot on the Monterey Jazz Festival. I decided to play Bobby's songs again and was asked to perform at the Monterey Golf 'N' Jazz dinner hosted by Clint Eastwood. I was told that Clint would likely stay for about five minutes and not to be offended when he left.

Eastwood entered and sat down front, about five feet from where I stood. I fought back nerves as he set that infamous Dirty Harry scowl upon me. Clint is a jazz superfan, director of documentaries on Dave Brubeck and Charlie Parker and a damn good pianist himself. Once he left, the pressure wouldn't be so much. Then again, I really, *really* hoped he would stay.

Clint didn't move. He stayed for my entire set.

The next year, Bobby and I geared up to make a second record together. I wanted to step up production values and make it a memorable, "big moment" experience for us both. We checked out a couple of local studios but didn't find the feel we were looking for. But there was one other studio I had heard about....

Bobby and I drove up to Nicasio, a little township in Marin County, and entered the gates into George Lucas's Skywalker Ranch. A mist hovered over Lake Ewok, a massive Victorian mansion with wraparound porch reflecting on the water. High on a hilltop, an observatory was perched to search the stars while statues of Yoda and Indiana Jones watched over the gardens.

It felt like the set of some grand movie—but it was all real. There was a vineyard and organic farm, with a chef to prepare meals for the guests. Skywalker Studios typically did film scores, but we were able to experience our own little brand of Lucas magic there and Bobby was giddy over their nine-foot Yamaha Concert Grand.

Natalie Cole's pianist, Josh Nelson played on our tracks and Leslie Ann Jones was the engineer. Leslie had a shelf full of Grammys and had worked with everyone from B.B. King to Alice in Chains. We called the album *Don't Move* and had so much fun that a year later, we chose Fantasy Studios in Berkeley, another incredibly famous studio, for Bobby to perform a record of his own compositions.

At age eighty-two, it was time.

CHAPTER TWELVE

GAINING MOMENTUM

"SMILE"

When you grow up being called worthless by your mother, you're always looking for validation and trying to prove yourself. Despite an overflowing plate, I took a part-time position as marketing director for the Jazzschool in Berkeley. I worked on their marketing and social media presence which back in that day, consisted of MySpace and email campaigns. At the same time, I taught a course on publicity, basically coaching musicians on how to get people to show up for their performances. It felt good to know I was successful enough that a school like the Jazzschool would hire me to share advice.

I enjoyed encouraging other musicians, but only ended up staying about a year. The school was resistant to technology at that time, and I knew it wasn't my calling anyway. I didn't want to talk about performing—I wanted to perform.

I was at that place in adulthood where you try to be thankful for the things that are going right without obsessing over the parts that are still a mess. But also, without being in denial or so delusional that you avoid working on your issues. Career-wise, life was good. I was playing shows and making records and my friendship with Bobby Sharp was rewarding on a professional and personal level.

On the other hand, Greg and I had parted ways and soon enough, I found myself stuck in one of those toxic relationships that seems so confusing, the kind that keep you forever second-guessing yourself and asking, *is this love or dysfunction? Do I hold on or let go? Am I the crazy or sane one here?* Ugh. The endless spin cycle of ugh.

Plus, Bennett was going into junior high. Tweens start looking for affirmation from peers rather than parents. They start to push back more and cling less. They say things like, "Can't you just drop me off here and not come in to Madison's party?"

In Little Miss B's case, she didn't want me coming to her parties because apparently, I was the "cool mom" and got in the way of her having fun. I suppose that made the lonely drive home a little easier? Not really.

I don't know how I figured out how to be a mom. I was scared that I'd end up being abusive like my mother was to me.

It took several sessions with a good therapist before she was able to convince me that I would not go down that road.

I raised Bennett to be creative and independent and we always spoke openly about sex. Long before she hit puberty, I let her know what to expect and what parts went where. Problem is, Bennett would then share this information with her classmates. Some of her friend's mothers begged me to make her stop.

One mother at a parent's night out that included the consumption of red wine and a bit of knitting said quietly, "Umm, I know you're really open about everything with Bennett, but could you tell her not to tell Ashley? We're not there yet."

Well, I did ask Bennett not to talk to her school friends about sex. But I can't guarantee that Ashley didn't get the full scoop anyway. You never tell a kid NOT to do something if you don't want them to do it.

A little further into her teens, Bennett started dating a boy. I sat her down and made sure she understood that even in the midst of all the confusing intersections of love, hormones, and sex—I believed her feelings were completely valid. It's wrong to trivialize someone's experience just because they are young.

"If you're ever considering having sex, just let me know," I told her. "I'll help you get an appointment to get on the pill or buy you some condoms. Just tell me. I'd rather know."

"Mom, why the hell would you need to get me condoms?" Bennett replied. "I can get them myself."

She said this straight-faced and with total confidence. I didn't know whether to hug her or cry. I'd be embarrassed to buy condoms even now. I gently suggested that I thought that sex is better with someone you love, and that it wasn't something to take lightly. But I told her that was just my opinion.

A few months passed and we were walking on the beach. A gentle wind was at our backs and the kite-surfers were out in throngs. I always loved any one-on-one time with Bennett, but walks with her by the water were the absolute best.

"Okay, so I'm maybe thinking about having sex with this boy," Bennett said.

The blood pulsed to my temples as I tried to keep from falling in the sand. I wanted to be cool, but inside, my anxieties were at a freak-out code red. Talking to your kids about theoretical sex is a lot different than the distinct possibility of sex. I guess there's a parental part of you that is never quite ready for that.

I didn't want to blow it though. I'd promised myself to support and not judge and ultimately, Bennett made the decision for herself that it wasn't time.

Bennett and I also talked openly about alcohol and drugs. I knew she would be offered liquor and weed at some point, and I could still remember the pressure to fit in, the burning curiosity to try illicit things. Cigarettes were non-negotiable though. That's where I drew the line.

Other than that, why stick my head in the sand? I wanted Bennett to feel like she could talk to me about anything. She's going to try drinking, probably smoke a joint. Just don't feel like you have to lie to me about it, okay?

In high school, Bennett would head out for a night with friends dressed in an assortment of what most people would consider not fashionably ideal. Patterns, colors and fabrics mixed. Rarely what anyone else was donning but completely acceptable Bennett-style. Sometimes it would be a dress from a consignment store and one of my faux furs. Other times it was the tightest-fitting skinny jeans and a "dad-sweater." I'd offer something like, "Have a good time, love. Don't get shit-faced!"

In other words, a little curiosity is a normal part of being a teen, but don't get so wasted that you made bad decisions or put yourself in a vulnerable position. Respect yourself, always. Did it work? I think so. Bennett would come home, and I'd ask how the night went, if she'd had anything to drink.

"Yeah," she'd reply casually, "Erin had some vodka in a water bottle. I took a few sips."

Or another time she told me, "I tried smoking some pot, but I don't think it did anything."

I would tell her to drink plenty of water, brush her teeth and get into bed. And I would always thank her for being honest with me. No lecture. No punishment.

I didn't drink much, I never had the taste for it, or do drugs (I didn't want to die!), so she never felt like I was giving her permission or encouragement to get drunk or high. Bennett just knew she could try these things and not get torn down by me afterwards.

Letting go is scary, but that's part of being a parent. It was a small price to pay to build our trust. Kids grow up and spread their wings. Liberating? Sure. Heartbreaking? Yeah, of course.

Maybe it was time to spread my wings too.

I found a twelve-week online course at Boston's Berklee School of Music on entrepreneurship. It's almost a cliché—musicians are notoriously bad at business. But I had a hunger for business. I was pretty good at it. And I wanted to get better.

Our professor was Chris Stone, who had an MBA from UCLA and was co-founder of The Record Plant in New York City. It's one of the most famous studios in the world. Maybe *the* most famous. *Electric Ladyland. Purple Rain.* Springsteen, *Born to Run.* Beastie Boys, *Paul's Boutique.* Fleetwood Mac's *Rumours,* The Allman Brothers, *American Pie.* Too many superstar platinum records to even name.

Initially, I wanted to apply the knowledge to all my businesses, the record label, publishing company, and my booking agency. Stone helped me realize that I needed to focus on one thing, so I chose my agency, Entire Productions. In 2007, I was a solo entrepreneur and sole proprietor, with no employees. Entire allowed me to have a life and career around music, but I didn't consider it a business that I was ever going to grow. I was still looking for that big lottery-winning major label record deal.

Chris Stone taught us about marketing and how to make a business plan, focusing on the essential elements. Executive summaries, financial forecasts, assessments of strengths and weaknesses, price/fee structures. I soaked in all this information and for the first time, felt I was moving my business in a true direction. Instead of flying by the seat of my pants, I started making a plan. Improv is a key skill for jazz players, but you don't want to run your business that way.

There were a few small to mid-sized entertainment production agencies in the Bay Area at this time. The concept of branding and target demographics was exciting, and I felt confident that I could take the information I was learning and make my mark in the local market. I liked having to craft an "elevator pitch" and identify our "competitive edge."

"What makes your business unique?" Stone asked one day.

Most agencies had the same old tired roster of talent that most everyone had already seen at the same old tired parties and events. I had my ear to the ground and was always searching for new, cutting-edge talent. And I wasn't just some "agent." As someone who had been playing and booking gigs since high school, I could coordinate talent and enable event planners to concentrate on all of the other elements. Still, I knew I had a lot left to learn.

I decided to dive deep and do a proper relaunch of my company. New logo and website, new ideas, new ways of thinking. I hired graphic designers and copywriters. Presentation is key, but aesthetics cannot be camouflage for shoddy work. The culture of social media has created a world of smoke and no substance. The work speaks loudest in the end. That which endures has substance. Build your life work on anything else, and it will fade like smoke in the wind.

Towards the end of the course, Chris Stone told me that I was one of his best students. To get that sort of recognition from someone of his stature gave me a huge shot of confidence and honestly, I needed it. In some ways, I was still the girl from 29th street in Des Moines, the kid who picked scabs and wore thrift store clothes, who had been kicked out of her house at sixteen and barely finished high school.

I had skipped around to three different colleges but never graduated and most of the doors that had opened for me were due to violin. But Mr. Carlson said I was a "natural"—so did that even count? Perspective is a hard thing to get sorted in your own head.

Shortly after Stone's class, I rented a space in San Francisco from a struggling magazine. It really was just a "space"—a desk in a room full of other working people. I started hiring part-time help, got my class information together and jumped in the only way I knew how—work my ass off. Not only working hard but working smart, getting more done in less time. I expected that from those who I hired and made sure they never saw anything less from me.

Most of my employees were efficient on their own, and those who weren't didn't last. But the ones who stuck around and thrived made me feel more successful and helped me get the word out about my new company. As Bennett transitioned into high school, I started getting out and about town a lot more myself.

At first, we stuck to booking jazz and classical groups for social and corporate events but as the business grew and obtained bigger clients, I started working with acts like magicians and balloon twisters. Then, we added DJs, models and dancers.

Entire Productions was going so well that I decided to throw a launch party. We had four caterers, aerialists flying overhead as a Motown band played "Papa Was a Rolling Stone" and everybody danced. A wizard wandered through the tables doing magic tricks, clowns juggled fire, we even had a photographer taking headshots and an old-time photo booth set-up for our guests to do silly, fun pics. Not only was our event a smash—it showed off what my company was all about and sent the message—hey, we can make *your* event look like this too.

Holidays have always been a struggle for me. Instead of joy and cheer, Christmas is mostly riddled with fear, anxiety and bad memories. The highlight for me that year was doing a Christmas Eve show at Yoshi's, so I decided to release a proper holiday record called *The Season*. We recorded most of the tracks live and did a song of Bobby's called "As the Years Come and Go." My dad recited "'Twas the Night Before Christmas" over my band riffing on Vince Guaraldi's *Charlie Brown Christmas* theme. Couldn't hurt to start making better memories to associate with the holidays.

My version of "Unchain My Heart" from the *I Had a Feelin'* record was selected for the soundtrack of *The Bank Job* with Jason Statham that year. We didn't even have a song plugger pitching our tunes for movies or television shows. The producers found my recording on their own. It wasn't Broadway, but I'd made it to the big screen.

I kept making records, branching out, even covering the classic "Blue Skies" with Oakland rapper Dublin on the track. Bobby Sharp and I were still a pair, singing here and there, working on songs. He had become a trusted friend to Bennett and me, like family.

I continued to keep a full plate of producing records and playing shows. Doing music while running a company started to wear me down. I felt like I'd made my mark and it was time to step away from music and focus on business instead.

Then, tragedy struck again.

CHAPTER THIRTEEN

EMPTIEST NEST

"DON'T SET ME FREE"

At eighty-seven, Bobby was getting frail, but we were still playing music together and he kept on sharing stories and helping me direct my life. We'd been best of friends for nearly a decade, and it never occurred to me that anything could ever happen to him. Then the doctors found a sarcoma on the inside of his elbow and gave him the choice of radiation or losing his arm.

"I think I'm just gonna let 'em cut it off," he told me.

"I don't think amputating the arm of a piano player is a good idea at your age," I replied. "So that's a hard *no*."

Bobby sighed and stubbed out his cigarette with a weary smile. "Yeah," he agreed. "I guess you're right."

The treatment team set Bobby up for a six-week regime of radiation treatments and I drove him over to get zapped almost every day. We would take the long way around the Bay to Oakland, windows down, laughing and listening to the music we'd made together. Bobby would sing along, telling and re-telling the stories behind the songs, talking about growing up in Harlem, Sammy Davis Jr. and Quincy Jones, the night he wrote "Unchain My Heart" on a Wurlitzer organ in his parents' apartment, how he kicked a heroin habit on his own.

I don't know why it takes the thought of possibly losing someone to make us appreciate them more, but I am thankful for those moments. They were truly the best of times.

One afternoon, my dad called to say he'd taken Bobby to the hospital after a bad fall. The physicians gave him another choice: have surgery on his broken leg or lay flat for nine weeks to let it heal. Bobby had given me power of attorney to make medical decisions, but before I could arrive to help, he chose to do the surgery.

Bobby had a fear of being sick and helpless. "If things go bad, don't let them resuscitate me," he had told me more than once. "I don't wanna linger when it's my time to go."

The surgery did not go well. Bobby was struggling to regain consciousness and after a few days his doctor asked me to consider palliative care. We moved him to a quiet room. I was afraid I was letting him down, not following his wishes, letting him linger in suffering and pain.

We'd been at the hospital a long time and my dad told me to take a break and get some air. I walked down to the closest Starbucks, rehearsing options, wondering what to do. When I returned, the nurse told me that Bobby didn't have much longer.

"Already?" I asked, in shock. "Oh...."

It was only the three of us in the room. We had a CD player there and I put on the record we had made together. Bobby opened his eyes. The song's long refrain began, and just as he used to hold those sweet, high notes forever, he held his eyes on mine, speaking something more than words could say, love and thanks and still something more.

I placed my hand on top of his. No words were needed. The look between us was enough. *Goodbye, my friend.* In whatever place there is beyond this world of confusion and loss and pain, I hope to see you there. I will meet you in that place where the music will never, ever end.

As the song faded, Bobby closed his eyes and died.

Bobby passed away in January of 2013 and Bennett left for college at SMU in Dallas that spring. With Bennett and Bobby both gone, the nest felt empty to say the least.

Entire Productions was slowly growing but nothing could replace the loss of my two closest companions. Bobby left me the rights to his music catalog and for the first time in my life, I had some money.

I bought a cute 600 square foot apartment in San Francisco and decided to try to have some fun as a single woman. Relive my lost youth a bit? Maybe so. I signed a singer/songwriter named Tim Hockenberry to Poignant Records and hired my brother Justin to arrange and produce his album. Justin ended up playing most of the instruments on Tim's record too. Music runs in our blood.

America's Got Talent would call me every so often looking for musicians, and I sent Tim their way. Howard, Howie and Sharon Osbourne loved his gravelly voice, and he made it all the way to the semifinals before being voted out. Though Tim was attractive, we never went on a date. I knew better by that point.

Mom resurfaced. Thom had died a few years earlier and she had stopped paying her bills. The bank foreclosed on her house, and she couldn't work so my brothers and I moved her out to Alameda. It was California or out on the streets. Was I seriously complaining about an empty nest?

I signed the lease and paid for a U-Haul truck to pack her belongings in. Justin went back to Iowa, packed all her things in the U-Haul, and drove them back to California.

Things had been tough for my mom. She'd battled stage four ovarian cancer years back and endured multiple surgeries, including a botched procedure which left her in constant pain. She became addicted to Oxycontin and in addition to her mental problems, now had an army of physical problems as well. Her hair had receded to the back of her head. She gained weight, lost her front teeth, and wore an orthopedic boot due to neuropathy from the chemo.

Despite all the hell she had put me through, I didn't want to see her suffering. But I didn't feel like I could afford to get tangled back up in dysfunction either.

I threw myself into work to deal with grief and the new maturity that going through difficult life changes brings. Technology was booming and I wanted to take Entire Productions to a higher level with a new approach.

So, I created a new system. Let's say someone calls for help with their wedding. They want to hire a string quartet for the ceremony and a band for the reception. Every time I talk to that client, it's captured by my software. Need to change the time? Don't want the musicians seen by guests until the performance? Trying to surprise the bride with a fire-breathing clown? It's all in the system.

Wedding details are all a little different but overall, the ceremonies are largely the same. Every event has common factors so why not streamline the process? Personalize the personal and let tech handle the things that are basically identical. I created those automations and five years later, we did 777 events with only two people in operations.

I was on a roll and wanted to keep pushing and learning new things. My friend Rebecca's husband, Doug, was doing a program for small businesses at Babson College sponsored by Goldman Sachs. After their nightmare role in the financial crisis of 2008, Goldman put a five hundred-million-dollar fund together to help smaller companies grow. (Or at least that's why I think they developed the program....)

I signed up and we met from nine in the morning to nine at night, businesses of every kind, from all over the country:

Industrial construction and ice cream shops, country doctors and car wash chains. Nobody else there was booking acrobats and Beatle tribute bands, though.

Regardless of our fields, we all had similar challenges, and by putting us together we could share information and help each other along. I knew marketing, branding and communications, but spreadsheets and financial reports made me break out in hives. Mike Fetters, our finance teacher, would throw out terms like "P&L Reports" and "EBITDA" and call on me to participate. I felt completely lost and in over my head.

We all feel like fish out of water sometimes, but I knew that if I pressed on instead of running, I could figure it out and it wouldn't be so scary. Turns out EBITDA simply stood for **E**arnings **B**efore **I**nterest, **T**axes, **D**epreciation, and **I**nterest. Essentially, your net income. Okay, that I could understand.

I had been trusting my gut on a lot of things—and doing well with it—but once your company starts growing, gut instinct alone won't cut it anymore. Eager to implement my new knowledge, I would send the incoming info to my handful of employees. "Change this plan," I would tell them. "Stop doing that and start this."

A lot of it is common sense, once you turn the lights on. Learn and teach others. Keep the river flowing. Delegate. Think big. Share. Balance instinct and stats. Know when to run and when to be still.

The idea began to spring up that I could really do well with my business. Entire Productions could become much bigger than me.

CHAPTER FOURTEEN

BE THE CONDUCTOR WHEN YOU CAN

"AT LAST"

After Babson's program, I had a new set of tools to help Entire Productions scale up. Now, to put those tools into motion. The high-level executive of a large and influential company was a friend and happy to offer advice. "What do you want, Natasha?" Scott asked. "A new house? Beamer? Vacation in Turks and Caicos?"

"No, I don't care about any of those things," I replied.

"So, what motivates you?" he said.

"I want to take care of me and my brothers after we can't work anymore."

"Well, that's retirement."

Turns out I didn't have much put back for that. Scott said I'd need to start saving more. A lot more. He also suggested I wasn't charging nearly enough for Entire's services.

I didn't want to gouge anyone. I wanted to be fair, and maybe, some of what was driving my reluctance was the need to be accepted and liked. But I trusted Scott and he said to raise prices until we got pushback. So, I did, and Scott was right. Our revenue grew by seventy percent.

At the time, AAA was launching their first new product since 1971, the Gig car-share program. Scott's colleague, Jared, called me to help plan their event. "If you're looking to hire entertainment, we're the right company for you," I explained. "Otherwise, you need to call an event planner. There are three local and they're all capable. I can give you their numbers if you'd like."

"No, we want you to do it," Jared said.

"But we're not event planners!" I replied.

Two days later, I was having breakfast with Scott. "When are you going to call Jared back?" he asked.

"For what?"

"Natasha, *you* are going to plan our event," he said. "We're just waiting for you to realize it. Why give that revenue to someone else?"

It made sense when Scott put it that way. AAA wanted to throw a launch party for six thousand people, with three parade routes for their new fleet of Gig cars, so I dove right into planning, and it was SO COOL! On a picture-perfect day full of Bay-area sunshine, we did morning yoga, threw a sober rave, and set the world record for most musical performances ("gigs") in a car. Sax players in the back seat, dreadlocked guitarists singing Bunny Wailer from the passenger side. Drummers and trombonists, accordion players, banjo pickers, and performers from every genre.

We decorated AAA's Gig cars to the hilt and choreographed it so the musicians would jump out at specific stops on the parade to entertain the crowd. Thousands of people turned out and everything went off perfectly on time and in tune. With laughter and music buzzing around me, I realized that event-planning was a lot like conducting a symphony. You don't always have to follow the band—be the conductor when you can.

As crazy and complicated as a Gig-car parade sounds, Entire Productions was able to take this idea to the next level and make it a one-of-a-kind event because my staff is as "Type-A" as I am: super- competitive, highly organized, maybe a little nutty sometimes.

Look, we've all got quirks. The trick is making your quirks work for you instead of against you. Easy-going people are probably not the best choice for planning your wedding or your company's launch party. You want a meticulous and hyper-driven team on the job.

From there, we were off and running, planning big, exciting events for companies like Apple, Google, Microsoft, Netflix, Paramount, and the Super Bowl, knee-deep in every part of the process, from sourcing the venue to picking out the color scheme and themes. Our definition of entertainment also expanded to include cigar bars, casino tables, crafting tables, comedians, dancers, and clowns.

Not long after AAA's event, we were hired to put together a big after-party at a San Francisco nightclub based on the "Seven Deadly Sins." The company gave us total carte blanche with two restrictions: NO FIRE AND NO EXOTIC ANIMALS.

No problem!

Models were dressed in elaborate costumes and painted up to represent each of the seven deadly sins, wandering the floor so guests could dance and mingle with Envy and Pride. Except for "Sloth" who was draped in moss and cobwebs and melted into a chair. A Black Swan ballerina with zombie eyes welcomed guests at coat check while an aerialist spiraled down from the ceiling on a long silk scarf. At one point I was bustling around, making sure everything was in order, and walked in on our body painter touching up the inside of Lust's butt.

Tash, you're not in Iowa anymore, I thought. *This sure beats waiting tables back in Des Moines.*

Here's a good one: Once, we got a call for the birthday celebration of an eighty-year-old Jewish woman. She wanted male strippers backflipping out of their chaps while wearing blinking Star of David necklaces.

"Absolutely not," I told her. "One-hundred percent, no way."

Then we surprised her and did it, of course. Did I mention my job is fun?

More companies started putting on wildly adventurous and interactive events, so instead of simply calling Entire an "entertainment production company," I revamped our motto to reflect the times: *We create bold experiences that drive guest engagement and brand evangelism.*

But wild is not enough. Each event must be well-thought out and in designing an event, we began to carefully consider the psychology of our client. If we're throwing a party for Microsoft, we need to understand that tech programmers are probably not going to want to dance and socialize all night. They'd much prefer to do a scavenger hunt on a pirate ship or play a full-sized real-life version of Pac-Man.

I'm proud I can employ people in full-time jobs with benefits. Struggling to make it on minimum wage and tips, living paycheck to paycheck, praying you don't get sick because you don't have insurance—I've been there. Employees are the lifeblood of any successful company, and I search for grounded, hard-working people with a positive attitude and common values.

If they also share a passion for music, events, and the arts, that's a bonus, but finding the right people is more difficult to describe than that. It's a sixth sense that develops over time, a chemistry of who fits, a balance of work ethic and of not taking oneself too seriously—the kind of people you'd want by your side whether there's a party on the boat or the ship is going down.

I don't always get it right. There were employees I felt certain would be stellar who let me down and others who soared I swore would flop. But those who fit are *so* worth it.

I want my people to help guide the company's path. An outside perspective can be liberating. If you aren't learning from your staff, you've let ego get in the way.

Trust your people and let them go. I'm incredibly flexible, as long as things get done. Work when you want, where you want.

Each month, I ask my employees to fill out a milestone sheet, listing achievements that go above and beyond their job description. I encourage my team to ask for raises and title changes. Sure, my expectations are high, but I am also their biggest supporter, and I make sure to acknowledge those who contribute, every way that I can.

Let's learn and grow, together. I'll even pay for it. Entire Productions has one employee I've spent thousands on—but every time I send her to a seminar or class, she comes back better than before. Invest in your people. Take care of them and your reputation as an employer will grow.

As my company began to prosper, one of the first things I focused on was defining our Core Values—*Collaborative, Excellence, Growth-Minded, Own It*, and *Scrappy*. The purpose of core values is to show employees, artists, and clients what we stand for and what to expect when working with us. I don't lecture my team. I serve as their example and in turn, they should serve as examples for each other.

Our employees need to *own their behavior*. If we make a mistake or if one of our artists screws up, we need to own up to it before we hear it from the client. And we need to apologize and offer them something in return for our error. That's how we make a client feel valued. If you own your behavior and are honest, you will succeed far more than people who try to cover their mistakes.

Owning one's behavior really became a core value when I started to delegate. Employees need to learn how to calm a nervous musician and get him out onto the stage, listen to a panicked caterer and calm the waiters when we're all in the weeds. Delegating is what allows people to find their sweet spots. It's more productive to work *on* your business than *in* the business day-to-day. These days, I rarely interact one-on-one with clients. I'm more of a strategist, visionary, and cheerleader.

When a client contacts my company, we respond quickly with an idea of substance, not just an empty response thanking them for their email and saying that we'll get back soon. Excellence is never static. It is about doing your absolute best within every changing moment, in every changing situation. No one is perfect. Anyone can be excellent.

As for scrappy, well, that's just taking a bootstrap mentality to everything you do. I want to work with people who are committed, humble, hungry, who have grit. Scrappy is the only way I ever knew how to live. It's what got me through tough times, through teen shelters and no place to live, no money, nobody to look after me. I always had to fight. The alternative is to lay down and quit.

And I would never quit.

We had Thanksgiving 2018 at Jeremy's. My mother showed up. I had not laid eyes on her since the previous Christmas. She shuffled into Jeremy's apartment, anxious, prattling, and nearly toothless, wearing a denim button-down and silver link bracelet with a silver turquoise ring. Her hair was past her waist and still predominantly black with grey patches in the front.

Emotions rushed through me, shame, fear, anger. I felt sorry for her. But also embarrassed. And scared that I could end up that way. Then I was angry for having such superficial feelings.

I should have been the bigger person instead of judging her just as she had always judged me. Once again, I felt the pressure to act like everything was okay. My mother was verbally and physically abusive. Her constant hatred and threats messed up my head and feelings of confusion and worthlessness hounded me for a long, long time. Sometimes, they still do.

Rage towards my mother played a large part in my motivation to succeed and prove her wrong. I wanted to go beyond self-sufficiency, to be a verifiable success. Motivation to rise above usually requires an opposing force, an enemy, but you grow up and figure out this is not the healthiest way to build a life. You might conquer your own personal Mt. Everest, you might even plant your flag, but there's not a lot of peace and joy in doing so. One of the things success teaches you is that true wealth is peace of mind.

Sitting at Thanksgiving dinner with my mother, dad and brothers made me realize that I had given all those horrible memories far more power than I should have. If hurt and pain were powering my success, then I would always have to keep them near me. I could never let go.

After dinner, we headed out to see a movie together. The lights went down and there we were, just like when I was a kid. My mother, my dad, my two brothers and me.

My mom had become more docile in her old age, but I knew that she was not kind to my brothers, even as they tried so hard to help. I held that as my last vestige of bitterness and resentment. I knew I would never get a lengthy apology from her. I'm not even sure she was capable of understanding how much her behavior had wrecked our lives. But maybe I didn't need that anyway.

It was raining after the movie, so I decided to take a rideshare back home. I didn't want my dad to have to drive all that way from Alameda to San Francisco and needed some time to myself anyway. Lyft never would respond so I finally tried Uber. Fifteen minutes later, I was still waiting for a ride. My phone rang and it was my mom.

"Are you okay?" she asked. "It's raining hard and you're standing out there all by yourself waiting."

The concern in her voice caught me off-guard. In her own, twisted, messed-up, broken, way, she was trying her best to express love. I wanted it. Maybe I even needed it. But I was not able to receive it.

"I'm okay," I assured her. "I'm waiting in the theatre lobby now. My ride will be here soon. Thanks."

The rain came down in sheets on the Alameda sidewalk. I stared at the rows of movie posters as melted butter drizzled over slowly popping corn. Finally, a green Kia Soul pulled to the curb and my phone dinged to say Omar had arrived. I rode home in the back seat, silent, staring out the window at the rain.

CHAPTER FIFTEEN

KEEPING SECRETS

"DOIN' THE IMPOSSIBLE"

I joined a group for entrepreneurs, *Entrepreneurs' Organization*, and learned that there was a highly sought-after program I could apply to at MIT—an Entrepreneurial Master's Program, or EMP for short. Prospects had to write an essay and submit a video to apply. Out of hundreds of applicants, only 65 are chosen from around the world. But I was good at those things. I had been auditioning most all my life. Sure enough, I got accepted to the program. Pretty good for a kid from Des Moines who didn't even have a college degree.

When our home life sucks, we make a family of our own. I realized that's what I had been doing all along. Symphony is a family. Choir is family. Restaurant workers are a family. Sure, they can be just as dysfunctional and fumbling and conflict filled as every other family in the world, but still. We make our own families. And if you do it right, a company can be family too.

I wanted to do everything I could to nurture and teach and make sure that Entire Productions was the best kind of family. I don't expect perfection. Perfect is the enemy of good. Let's just all be smart, informed, and do our very best to be excellent.

In April 2019, Justin and I were having dinner at the Asian fusion place in Union Square, talking about the things siblings discuss, challenges we faced as kids, parents getting older, how hard it is to feel happy and whole given how we grew up. Our talks had taken on a new depth after I told him I was writing a book.

Justin stirred the rice with his chopstick, not saying much for a while. Finally, he broke the silence. "I have something I need to tell you."

The tone of his voice told me something heavy was on the way. I sat up straight and waited for the bomb to drop.

"When mom went in for surgery for ovarian cancer, she thought she might die. She told me that when she was eighteen, she had a daughter and had to give her up for adoption. She gave me all the information she knew and said, 'If I don't make it, you could look for her.'"

My mind spun, searching for an anchor point. It felt like he was speaking a different language.

"Tash," Justin said. "We have a sister."

Mom made it through surgery and wanted to sweep it all back under the rug. Justin had carried the girl's information in his wallet for nearly twenty years. We had a sister. *I* had a sister. Out there, somewhere.

Justin handed me a piece of paper. It was yellowed and worn, folded and re-folded many times. "I'm going to find her," I promised. "And I'm going to do it within twenty-four hours. Nothing is going to stop me."

After scouring adoption websites and nearly a thousand profiles of people searching for their biological families, I found a potential match. I called my dad to get his side.

"Yes, you have a sister," he sighed. "But it was your mother's place to tell you that."

I called the woman I found. Her name was Nicole and she lived in Texas. The adoption agency had changed her name and she wasn't sure we were kin, but a DNA test proved we were long-lost siblings. Nicole is biracial, which was taboo in the 60's-era Midwest. My mother kept her for about a year, following the father from state to state. At some point, she had no choice but to place Nicole up for adoption.

I don't know what kind of mental issues my mom has, but I am still the mother of a beautiful baby girl, and I cannot imagine the thought of raising her for a year and having to let go. Whether manic depressive or schizophrenic or even if you were healthy and relatively well-adjusted—giving up your year-old baby would truly wreck a person's heart and soul.

As shocking as the news was for me, imagine how my sister felt when I called out of the blue. I gave her my mom's contact information and Nicole reached out, but my mom refused to respond. It sounds cold, but I had a company to run so I immersed myself in MIT's program. Or maybe I was just running from the massive wave of feelings.

In the middle of my time at MIT, Nicole called me, curious about our mother. I told her the truth about the kind of life I had growing up. I think she realized she'd dodged a bullet. Nicole was better off with her adopted family, who had treated her lovingly and well. If she needed any information beyond that, she'd have to get it from our mom. I didn't want to say anything that would turn Nicole against her. Maybe they could have a better chance.

Nicole pressed in until my mother finally agreed to meet with her. Justin had business in Texas, close to Nicole, so he called to see if my mom could come along. Nicole insisted that our mother stay at her home instead of a hotel. Given her mental and physical state, I'm not sure how profound their visit could be. My mom had told Nicole that she still had her long, beautiful hair and her life was amazing, that everything had turned out great. It didn't take long for my new half-sister to figure out she was not as picture-perfect as she had led her to believe but at least they were able to meet and spend some time together.

After their visit, my mother started acting out again, sending cryptic messages positioning my dad as the bad guy, trying to lay the blame on him for everything that went wrong. She was still capable of pushing my buttons.

"Even after all these years, you're still in an abusive relationship with your mom," Bennett told me.

Well, that was a shock to hear. But I realized it was true. Irrational? I don't know. Those old ghosts from childhood can haunt us long after we are grown. I found the best therapist possible and started sessions right away.

One of my mother's crazy emails said that if I wanted to know the real story about their attempt to have me committed to the psych ward, I should contact Broadlawns Hospital for transcripts. I did, and they sent Xeroxed copies of the doctor's notes.

> *Father fears patient will kill him in his sleep with butcher knife. Father recently out of rehab for alcohol. Patient doesn't understand why dad would bring her to mental hospital. States that she would never hurt him, was just frustrated. Patient is calm, well-kept, present. Patient's mother is on-site. Patient says mother hates her. Mother states she had a wonderful conversation with daughter and is not afraid of her killing or hurting anyone. Patient states she has never had a nice conversation with her mom.*

The psychiatrist spent a lot of time with me that day, trying to understand family dynamics and what was going on. When he decided to let me go, my dad became visibly upset, yelling and demanding that they admit me to the ward. Why the hospital let me return home with my parents is something I will never understand. Memory is a fragile thing. I guess I had always blocked that part out.

Not long ago, I called my dad on Facetime. Talking to my mother was pointless, but I knew I had to try and get some insight from him.

"Did you dramatize all that just to get me out of the house and out of harm's way?" I asked. "Were you trying to keep me safe by putting me in the hospital?"

"I can't remember all the details, but yeah, I think that was the case."

"Why didn't you ever try to stop her? Didn't you ever drive to work and think about how much she made our lives miserable?"

"Tash, I thought about it all the time. I just didn't know how to make her stop. I guess I was in denial about a lot of things. Back in that day, I had a large capacity for alcohol."

Even to this day, I don't call my parents "Mom" or "Dad." It's "my mom" or "my dad." That little extra "my" is less personal, and it makes me feel that much more independent. My dad messed up, but you grow up and figure out that your parents weren't perfect. Especially after you become one.

A lot of parents screw up their kids. But my father got a lot of things right. He took me to practice and rehearsal. He encouraged me in every way. He taught me to sing "Misty."

He was always there for Bennett. And he's here for me now.

While sorting through my personal drama, the business media started to take notice of Entire Productions. My dream was to make *Inc.*'s 5000 list of America's fastest growing companies. I saw a form in their magazine, so I crossed my fingers and sent in the application, along with three years of financial records signed by my CPA.

A few weeks passed. The mail carrier brought a big box to my desk. I opened it and balloons and confetti spilled out.

CONGRATULATIONS! The enclosed note said. *YOU MADE OUR LIST!*

I was so excited that I let out a huge yelp. My team dashed in to see if I had tripped over the rug or found a spider in my desk. Validation!

In the same year, *Entrepreneur* magazine listed me as one of the Top Entrepreneurial Businesses in America based on innovation, growth, leadership, impact, and business valuation. I was asked to speak at conferences and workshops, and we just kept increasing, faster and further than I had ever imagined. The entrepreneur program at MIT had gone so well that I applied to Harvard's as well and was invited to study onsite in Cambridge at Harvard's Business School.

I got to move back into the dorm. The *Harvard* dorms! I know you're not supposed to use a lot of exclamation points in writing, but I remembered struggling so much at KU, bouncing back to Iowa State, floundering and transferring yet again to Drake. I felt like I never would make it. So, MIT and now Harvard? Exclamation points are needed to fully express my feelings about that.

I flew out to Harvard in November, the campus covered with honey locusts and towering elms in bloom, a field of orange and yellow in the sky. Harvard's program pushed me further than ever before. Ivy League dreams require Ivy League dedication, so I jumped in, ready to work hard. I got to prepare and present my own case study, talking about licensing the system I had created for other companies to use. The group shot me straight about the pros and cons of such, all the things I would need to mull over before taking the next step.

While waiting in line for dinner one night, I checked my email. The team at *Inc.* wanted to know if I would speak at their *Fast Growth* event in San Francisco. Again, I couldn't believe they were choosing me. Out of all the businesses on their list they want me?

Of course, I said yes and was set to appear on stage with the owner of Birdies shoe company and the founder of Pandora music service. I met Brian Smith, who started the UGG boots company, and he even asked to take a selfie together. I felt like junior high jazz band opening for Fleetwood Mac, but after I spoke, there was a long line of people waiting to talk to me. That was pretty cool, maybe even the best part.

The acknowledgements kept coming. We made the *Inc.* 5000 for the third year in a row, *Entrepreneur* put us on their list again, the *San Francisco Business Times*' Top 100 Fastest Growing Companies in the San Francisco Bay Area, the Top 100 Women in Business, and we were also named one of the Top 50 Event Planners in the World by *Special Event* magazine. *BizBash* even named me one of their Top 500 event professionals.

"No limit" is something of a cliché, but I enjoy thinking big. I don't see a ceiling to what I can do anymore. I thought I had been put on this earth to be a musician. It was the only thing I was really any good at. But there was so much more.

And so much more remains. I am excited to learn, excited to change, excited to see what lies ahead.

"Hi, it's Natasha.
Here's a secret link
that I want you to check out.
www.therelentlessbook.com/secrets

I never thought that was possible for me. I felt like I was too damaged, too depressed, that no one could ever accept me like I was.

You know what "fake it till you make it" really means? It means, dammit, you are going to try. You do your best, even while you're still figuring it out. You're willing to learn, and you've realized the best way to do that is by diving into the deep end. It means that even if you're scared and unsure, you are determined not to let opportunity pass you by.

I started this book with a story about butcher knives and teen shelters, how my fantasy TV Christmas got ruined. We all want the storybook ending, but life rarely turns out that way. Usually, we have to take whatever closure we get and keep moving on.

My mother, the one person I should have been able to look to for encouragement and safety, hit me and called me bitch and threatened to kill me. My parents put me out and at age sixteen, I was on my own. I had to find encouragement and safety in other places. Mostly, I had to make things happen for myself.

Despite my upbringing, I managed to become a strong, successful woman. That's not to say I don't struggle. I still fight panic attacks and fits of despair, the feeling that regardless of how much I accomplish, it really doesn't matter because I will always be that seriously fucked-up kid that nobody loved enough to keep.

For years, I thought I had to keep my rage close, or I would lose the drive and ability to succeed, but as long as I kept digging up the past, the poison remained inside me. It was ugly, exhausting, and self-defeating in that most destructive secret place. I didn't want to stay stuck in that venomous cycle for the rest of my life so, at some level, I knew I had to let it go.

Everybody wants to make peace with the past. That doesn't mean we have to force some false sense of peace or let toxic people demolish our lives, even if they are family. My mother remains abusive. But it doesn't hit so deep anymore. Now, I just wait those feelings out. They're only feelings. I don't have to believe everything I think.

With respect to the cliché, I suppose I am still "faking it" because I haven't quite made it to where I need to be just yet. Do we ever? Human nature is to try and hide our flaws, but the only way you'll ever really help someone else is by letting them see your scars. That's one of the reasons I push. I know there are people out there going through the same kind of situations I did.

We don't have to be defined by our struggles. Struggle is what gives us the strength to rise above, and the humility to remain grounded.

CHAPTER SIXTEEN

DISGUISED OPPORTUNITIES

"BEFORE I DIE"

At the beginning of March 2020, Entire Productions was on track to do twenty-five percent more business than the year before. It felt like life was finally coming together for me in a lot of ways.

I hired a four-thousand-dollar-a-day coach to get a serious operating system in place for Entire and we were off with a bang.

When I started hearing news about a new virus going around, it didn't seem like it was going to hit that close to home. Various infectious diseases had popped up over the years and we'd certainly had crises but nothing that ever interfered with daily living to any large degree. We were neck-deep in planning Entire's annual marketing party and had over nine hundred people RSVP'd to attend, including contacts from our biggest clients like Airbnb, Google, and Twitter. The event was scheduled for March 17th and over the top in every way, six times bigger than it had ever been before.

Our theme for 2020 was "Into the Wild" and to be held at the California Academy of Sciences. We had two caterers, full bars, a West African Highlife band, and a DJ with an electric violinist who also sang. Every room was going to be filled with lights, entertainment, interactive activities, and our signature aerialists and body-painted models. For "Into the Wild" we were going to paint them up as zebras, rhinos, and lions.

Our upcoming bash was the talk of the industry. If a client were paying, an event of this magnitude would come at a price tag of over half a million dollars. Everything was sponsored, and those clients were counting on "Into the Wild" as their biggest marketing event of the year.

My team had worked tirelessly and even though news agencies showed clips of stranded cruise ships and crimson maps of viral spread, I promised everyone that we would go through with our event, as long as the venue was legally able to stay open. But then, when COVID started to creep closer, I made the decision to postpone the party for everyone's safety.

On March 16th, the day before our event was scheduled, the city of San Francisco gave the mandate for us to shelter in place. From there it all began to crumble, and things got crazy fast. In less than two weeks, my business went from a profitable multi-million-dollar company to zero revenue.

First, I got sick. Then, I got anxious. After that, I was anxious and sick. Like the panic ticker running at the bottom of news channels, the thought kept looping through my brain,

you are screwed . . . you are going to be homeless again . . .

. . . you are so screwed . . . you are going to be homeless again . . .

I could see myself, living in a doorway, hair matted, scratching for food. Or maybe I would end up in the Tenderloin, sleeping in a tent or a cardboard box. If you've ever been at rock bottom, there's a part of you that always fears going back there again. All these years later, I can still feel the dread of standing on the porch of a homeless shelter with my clothes in a garbage sack. I can still feel the anxiety of desperately calling friends and strangers, trying to find a place to crash, wondering *how* or even *if* I would make it through.

And I suppose there was still a part of me that feared I would end up like my mother.

As the plague hit harder, I went into full-on fight-or-flight mode. For all my rock bottoms, I had always found a way to scratch and dig and somehow, rise above. I remembered the times when I didn't even have enough money to buy Top Ramen at the grocery store, scraping by on my own ability to improvise. Working three jobs while going to school. Consumed by grief, but still moving.

Somehow, I just never quit. And if I had to do it again, it would suck and I would hate it and it would be scary and anxious and hard—but I would make a way, somehow. Maybe all that shit I had been through had a purpose after all. Either way, that was enough of the philosophy and contemplation. It was time to get to work.

Fortunately, I had built a strong network of mentors, so I reached out to ask what I should do about my company. My life wasn't the only one affected by the virus. I had twelve people on my team that depended on Entire Productions to make ends meet. After a lot of advice and consideration, I made the difficult decision to let five of my employees go.

I had a panic attack before I gave them the news but for the most part, they were understanding. Our industry was the first to be hit, and we were hit hard. In the weeks to come, thousands would join us in the suffering. Over 80 percent of the event industry was laid off, and a lot of businesses closed for good.

I still had no idea how bad the situation would become. They told us that lockdown would last two weeks but then two weeks passed, and things just got more insane, and nobody really seemed to know what was going on. I thought we might still have some revenue trickling in, but everything stopped, and I had to ask my remaining staff to go part-time or volunteer to be laid off.

There was no demand for live music or acrobats or catered food. No one could leave their house. And none of us had a clue when or if things would change. It was like all the apocalyptic terror of Y2K was finally coming true.

Lockdown gave me a lot of time to think about things. I realized that the best we can do with a bad situation is to try and pull the good from it. I'm not saying it's simple as making lemonade when life gives you lemons. But I had heard a lot of great businesspeople say their biggest triumphs came from hard times. There is always a lesson in the dark. Always something to learn. What is darker or harder than a worldwide plague?

Then again, what better place to make a fresh start?

The down time gave me the space to think about my business from a distance. I had been too busy to see the problems we were having. I thought about our million-dollar payroll and the taxes and benefits I was responsible for. Sixty-five thousand dollars a year in rent for an office space the size of a guest bedroom.

Was all that really necessary? Those of us who were still working were doing it from home and so far, at least in my experience, it was seamless. Once the anxiety settled down, my mind was buzzing with ideas. I split them into two columns, projects for now and projects to do later.

I began to think of ways to hold events that didn't rely on people getting together in person. Instead of a party, what if we presented a client's information in a variety show? With attention spans growing shorter with each passing year, we could do this in a fast-paced and entertaining way. This is when I went from panic attack to plan of attack.

I quickly devised a solution—shorter segments of information, keynotes, education bookended by entertainment and interactive elements that were no more than fifteen minutes each. Instead of sitting in front of a computer for an hour dying of boredom, we aimed to keep people alert, intrigued, and begging for more.

We were the first to market with this concept and I immediately presented it to the CEO of Mansueto Ventures that publishes both *Inc. Magazine* and *FastCompany*. I let our clients know what we were doing. It took a while for them to get on board, as I think they were still waiting to see if things would open up. They weren't as prepared as we were to do the pivot to virtual.

Until time passed and things became more frantic.

To speed up the process and make sure everyone knew what the experience could be like, we created our own virtual variety show with three main segments. It wasn't a demo, or a pitch, but rather an actual show that was informative, entertaining, and fun. Our project was a hit, clients started asking us to produce more virtual shows for their events, and we even picked up a few new ones along the way.

We got a good deal of press and lots of respect for the willingness to try new things in a difficult time. While the revenue wasn't anything close to pre-pandemic levels, it was certainly better than nothing. I believe virtual events will continue long after lockdown is over. The future of our business is virtual-only and hybrid virtual/in-person. That means that we now have a completely new division to potentially double our business once the pandemic is over.

I didn't want to waste the momentum so we began to reach out to our talent pool to ask what they could do in a virtual setting. Virtual is more than just doing your act live for the camera, it's knowing how to create your "set" with good lighting, a great microphone and quality camera work.

For some, it's how they translate their art to an audience behind a screen. Magicians, for example. How do you perform magic on Zoom? Entire has a magician we've used for years who is truly astounding.

"I'd love to send you some work," I said. "Can you perform on Zoom?"

"I don't have a virtual act," he replied. "And I never will!"

And . . . * *poof* *—just like that, one of our favorite magician/mentalists virtually disappeared.

But the amazing Kevin Blake was locked, loaded and ready to go. After appearing on our first variety show, we had multiple requests to hire him out—and he's blown them away every time.

Most entertainers love to work, and we've booked headline acts for a fraction of what they'd charge for a live, in-person event. Plus, it's a lot of fun to see a musician in a more stripped-down, authentic version of themselves, conversing with the guests on the screen as if they're long-lost college friends. Turns out people were longing for a more intimate setting all along.

Virtual is a permanent part of our culture now, even after people are able to gather in crowds. We even figured out a way to do virtual events for clients who don't have a need for entertainment. Sometimes it's a simple live chat format and other times we use a broadcast quality studio to produce a more polished affair.

Quarantine helped me fix things I didn't know were broken and forced me to brainstorm new ideas. I choose to believe those ideas will carry us higher than before. Optimism is powerful, but only when rooted in truth and practicality.

Jason Feifer, editor of *Entrepreneur* magazine, asked me to be a guest on his podcast, *Problem Solvers*, for the episode entitled, "Seeing Opportunity During the Coronavirus." This was early into the pandemic, and I was supercharged with thoughts on how to move forward. I probably came off as a bit manic and there was some measure of magical thinking, I'm sure, but in a sense, it was survival mode for me.

I'd experienced plenty of setbacks, tragedies and difficulties in my life and the only thing I knew to do was keep moving. Just keep figuring out some way to push ahead and make the best of a bad situation.

I told Jason that I refused to let myself sit still in quarantine. Instead of focusing on all the things I could not do—I would choose to concentrate on what I could. Things like workshops and books and programs to help other entrepreneurs. I could start on that while locked down in my apartment.

My song catalog had over seventy-five titles, including Bobby Sharp's tunes. Was I doing everything I could with this potential source of income? Bobby not only left me his music, but I also had twenty-four hours of videotaped interviews with him about his colorful life. Bobby worked with so many great entertainers back in the day. I'd love to get his story out there.

I began to think of my story too, all the places I had been, the things I had gone through. Maybe telling my story might help someone else along the way. Maybe there's another teenage kid out there somewhere who fears their life is beyond repair. But if I can get up and make something of myself, so can you.

The ideas kept coming. I thought back to a speech I gave for Salesforce's Dreamforce Conference. Once it was over, they handed me a hefty canvas bag loaded with goodies, a Bluetooth speaker, stickers, a grill set—all branded with the Salesforce logo. Everybody loves free treats and every event we did featured giveaways, so instead of ordering them from a third party, why not become the direct supply?

I applied for a resale license and before the board even approved it, I'd already sold forty-five hundred face masks custom branded with my client's logo. Which turned into an additional order of nine thousand masks and neck gaiters. We were in business! I snapped up the URL entireproductionsmarketing.com and created the website myself while my team created a look book of sample images.

It's strange how things turn out and lead you on a path you'd never consider. That same corporate client has a purchasing office that had to place the order for the masks. They don't know Entire as an event/entertainment company, but as a company that supplies goods. Could we provide them with three hundred thousand Nitrile gloves? No logos, no event, just for use in their internal workforce.

Can we?

I reached out to my network of business friends, found a connection with a source, and made the sale. So, I'm in the PPE business now? If I can be of service and keep my company afloat, then you bet I am.

It's easy to lay down and quit. Easy in the short run. Regret and lethargy are soul-killers. You can live with falling short if you know you put up a fight.

With a little success, my confidence returned. Theoretically, a nationwide lockdown should have been the end of a business that plans big gatherings. But I was finding ways to hold on and keep going.

I don't know what the future holds, but I feel like whatever comes my way, I'll be as ready as I can possibly be. It might be a cliché, but I can honestly say that the thing which did not kill me, really did make me stronger. I will always treasure this time when life forced me to slow down enough to rethink and reframe my priorities. And one thing I have found out for sure, I am my best self during a challenge.

I truly love what I do. It's never been about the money. The thrill of running a successful business is enough for me, especially one steeped in the arts, supporting musicians, helping people find their gifts, and enjoying the notoriety and reputation we have.

Entire Productions ended 2020 having produced over two hundred virtual events, one million in revenue and a tiny bit of profit. I received a notice from *Inc.* magazine that my company made their 5000 list for the third year in a row. This is based on 2019 numbers, so we'll be able to celebrate a big achievement during a very low-revenue year.

Ironic. But there's no way I'm letting it go to waste, I'm going to soak up every moment of it. My glass is always half-full and more than not, it's overflowing.

Bennett moved back to the Bay area after living in Los Angeles and Seattle following college. She's coming into her own as an artist, designing and making clothing and was offered a stint as a mask designer for a fashion brand in India and the U.K. called March Tee. They used Bennett's pattern and have her select the fabric. With an initial run of fifty thousand, it's not a bad start.

On Mother's Day, she gave me a hand-made card.

Thanks for treating me like a human with real emotions and opinions. You raised me to be independent, complicated, messy, and real and I have you to thank for the weird quirks and ability to ignore unrealistically serious social standards. I'm grateful that you are not only my mom, but also my best friend.

Bennett's note meant more to me than any gift, dinner or sappy store-bought Mother's Day card. Her words were my Grammy, my Pulitzer, and Nobel Prize. What I really wanted, was to break the chain of torment and abuse. To show love and not spew hatred, to give life and not threaten harm, to help my daughter become the best possible human she could be.

"Would it be okay if I told our stories in a book?" I asked her. "All of them, you, me, your grandmother, Aidan, your dad. Everything."

"Sure, why wouldn't it be?" she said. Same confidence. Same cool. "Put it all out there."

We never quite know how life will turn out. You sure don't know how your kids will turn out. You just do the best you can at the time. The entrepreneur awards and lists are nice but more important is the fact that my daughter trusts me. She can talk to me about anything, anytime.

That's a big win in my book. The kind that counts.

Oh yeah, *my book*. We're done, that's the end. For now, at least.

Writing a book is a long, strange process. You sit down and try to put all the pieces of your life in order, in some way that makes sense. I looked to a lot of people in the publishing industry for insight and guidance. If I'm doing something, I find the best teachers I possibly can. I am addicted to learning new things.

The book experts I consulted told me that it was important to tell your story as simply and straightforward as possible without confusing the reader. Easier said than done. Life is anything but simple and straightforward and so many parts are confusing still.

Did I succeed despite my upbringing—or because of it? Relentless tenacity will bring you some measure of success, but it can also make you crazy sometimes. I know that the difficulties I went through made me into the person I am today, but believe me, if I could go back and change things, I would've preferred to know the love and safety of my parents. I would not have been so lost and desperate and alone.

Who knows how things might have been different? Maybe I would be back in Iowa, married twenty-five years to the same person, first chair violin, Des Moines Symphony, grandkids coming, white picket fence.

Or I might be addicted or bankrupt now.

Adversity wrecks as many as it saves and success can be just as disappointing as failure. What ruins one, stirs another to rise above. We are both made and broken by the things that happen to us in our youth. Life is still so fucking weird.

And in many ways, I am still that scab-picking girl, standing in a dark room, staring out the window, trying to find my place in this world. My journalist friend down south says if you don't ponder and wrestle these feelings, can you truly say you have written a book?

The pieces of your life really do look different when you get it out of your head and onto paper, or a screen or whatever you use to read. Going into this, I thought I could write a book to help others change, to pass on what I had learned, to inspire people not to give up or let adversity steal your hopes and dreams. But the process ended up changing and inspiring me.

This is a story about a sad, scared, anxious kid from the Midwest who moved to California to try and make something of herself. I left Iowa as Tash and reinvented myself in San Francisco as Natasha, entertainer, entrepreneur, public speaker. (Author!)

But writing this book got me to thinking, maybe it's time to find Tash again.

It was late, on a Tuesday night. The process of writing was winding down. I took a virtual road trip through the streets of my hometown, back to Drake University and Spaghetti Works, to that cheap basement apartment I rented as a teen, to the old concert halls and school auditoriums, down past the ballfields where I was once so young and free, listening to the Violent Femmes sing let me go on....

Back to 29th Street, to the house where I grew up . . . the bay window with my mother's nails in my neck . . . the upstairs bedroom where I picked scabs and practiced violin . . . sitting on my father's lap, singing "Misty." All of it together, the good and bad, the pieces of a life.

This shit is hard, I thought.

But it's good. Things worked out okay. And maybe, in some strange way, it's supposed to be difficult. That's the price we pay for growing up and moving on.

I don't know what the future holds. None of us do. But whatever comes, I know I can handle it.

In fact, I'm looking forward to what's next.

CODA

THE TAKEAWAY

"THIS IS THE END OF A BEAUTIFUL BEGINNING"

What I hope you take from my story:

I had advantages and disadvantages. Good memories and bad, laughter and tears, highs and lows. Sometimes the low points worked in my favor and the highs worked against me. I was discouraged, disappointed, and did not always take the most direct path.

The key thing that helped me succeed was realizing the outcome was ultimately up to me. I had help, good friends and teachers, generous mentors—but it was my own refusal to give up that made the difference.

Your struggles may be far more or far less. That's not what's important. It's what you do today and tomorrow that counts.

Here are a few, final takeaways, lessons I learned along the way.

- Be willing to start ugly. Wait until things are perfect and you may never launch. Put it out there and redefine, mold and shape it along the way.

- Don't wait for help. Don't wait for someone to save you, fund you, or tell you what to do.

- You can come back from tragedy. You can overcome the damage done in youth. You can become a person at peace with where you are and who you are.

- Disappointment and disaster can be fuel to move you forward, but you can't lean on it forever.

- Be open to relationships with people outside of your normal circle or interest group. It might surprise you what happens.

- If you're depressed, stuck, bored or anxious, pour yourself into something outside of your routine. Draw. Play the piano. Go sailing, Hula hoop, make croquembouche, or ride a bike. It will distract you, lead to new discoveries, new ideas, and keep you from losing your mind.

- Bad shit happens. Learn from it, wait it out, and know that at some point in the future, you're likely to forget the pain that feels so overwhelming now.

- Don't overthink. Develop your gut instinct and learn to trust it.

- If you can't find a door, make your own.

- Not everything can be resolved. Sometimes it's best to walk away.

- There *are* shortcuts to success: Find a mentor. Take a class. Listen to the pros and study those who have gone before you.

- Realize that success can be every bit as stressful as failure.

- Everybody's got baggage. Do the best you can with what you have to work with.

THANKS

- Two12 Conference and Amber Rae for sparking and kick-starting this writing journey.

- Jamie Blaine- you made my #1 dream come true- my story in beautiful, gripping prose.

- Whitney Gossett, Amber Vilhauer/NGNG, Mike Alden for helping me get this book up, out and to the finish line and beyond!

- Jack Canfield, Patty Aubrey, Steve Harrison for direction, clarity and marketing direction.

- Bennett, Dad, Justin, Jeremy. Thank you for allowing me to tell this story.

- Didi D'Errico, Becky Donner, Jane Solomon, Victoria Sassine for being my incredible trusted readers and helping fill in the gaps and see my blind spots in the manuscript.

- Valerie- for caring for and feeding me.

- Cindy Kaczmarek and Tim Condon for your advice, friendship and for believing in me.

- To my team: Madeline, Thalia, Rachel, Patti.

- Thank you to the Entire Productions team!

NOTES

"If you are being harmed, need shelter or someone to talk to, please go to:

covenanthouse.org
nationalsafeplace.org
thehotline.org

ABOUT THE AUTHOR

Natasha Miller is the founder and CEO of Entire Productions, an event and entertainment production company based in the San Francisco Bay Area. She is a classically trained violinist and celebrated jazz vocalist. She is a graduate of the Goldman Sachs 10ksb program and has studied entrepreneurship at Harvard and MIT. Natasha is a 3x in a row Inc. 5000 honoree for having one of the fastest-growing businesses in the US. She is an advocate for homeless youth programs. Natasha is a proud mother of her daughter, Bennett, and lives in Oakland, CA. Find out more at OfficialNatashaMiller.com.

APPENDIX

Music available on iTunes, Spotify, Amazon, and Bandcamp

Natashamiller.bandcamp.com

PoignantRecords.com

EntireProductions.com

OfficialNatashaMiller.com

FascinatingEntrepreneurs.com

TheRelentlessBook.com

EMPOWERING ENTREPRENEURS TO
THRIVE, SCALE, & GROW
THEIR BUSINESSES
ONE PRESENTATION, CONVERSATION, & PODCAST AT A TIME.

Inspire your audience with actionable ideas for activating their business growth today by inviting Natasha to speak.

An Amazing Event Requires An Extraordinary and Entertaining Speaker Who:

- Engages the Audience
- Interacts with the Audience
- Relates to the Audience
- Empowers the Audience
- Entertains the Audience
- Takes the Audience on an Adventure

Natasha is just as comfortable speaking to an audience of 5 as she is to 40,000.

People are raving:

"KNOCKED IT OUT OF THE PARK"
"THE INSIGHTS YOU GAVE WERE PRICELESS"
"NATASHA IS A NATURAL STORY-TELLER"

OFFICIALNATASHAMILLER.COM/SPEAKING

NATASHA MILLER

SCALING BEYOND
YOUR FIRST MILLION™

...She's walked me through creating core values for my business and how to interview people and build my team. It has just been the most rewarding experience that has paid off tenfold. I couldn't recommend working with her more.
- ANNA DAVID, New York Times Bestselling Author, founder of Launchpad Publishing

This is a digital course for entrepreneurs who have at least $300k in revenue and 2+ employees who want to scale and grow their business by over 50% in a smarter, more efficient manner so that they can make more money and have more time to do the things they love outside of work.

OFFICIALNATASHAMILLER.COM

poignant records

Listen to and buy all of Natasha's recordings
including the Bobby Sharp catalog and other
artists on her label.

POIGNANTRECORDS.COM

Always thought of writing your own story? Inspired to start now?

Natasha created a guided course and book to get you well on your way to writing and publishing your own memoir.

> Natasha has been a great coach and resource to me while writing my book. Her step-by-step process helped me stay focussed and on track with content. She nudges at the right times. And she has a treasure chest of contacts--editors, publishers, promotional assistance--that saved me time and money.
> - STEPHANIE CAMARILLO, President, Entrepreneurs Organization, Idaho

MEMOIRSHERPA.COM

MEMOIR SHERPA

FASCINATING ENTREPRENEURS

WITH *Natalie Miller*

A PODCAST FEATURING INCREDIBLE + SUCCESSFUL ENTREPRENEURS

RATED TOP 1.5% IN THE WORLD

> *Achieve a higher level of success by tuning into Fascinating Entrepreneurs. Truly inspirational with insights that transform businesses and lives.*
> *- KAREN BRISCOE, Author*

Listen to the episodes to discover what makes the most successful and fascinating entrepreneurs tick... How do people end up being an entrepreneur? How do they scale and grow their businesses? How do they plan for profit? Are they in it for life or are they building to exit? These — and a myriad of other topics — will be discussed to pull back the veil on the wizardry of successful and fascinating entrepreneurs.

FASCINATINGENTREPRENEURS.COM

FOR BOOK CLUBS
DISCUSSION + EXPERIENCE

If you were coming to Natasha's home for a book club night, this is how she would plan for the experience.

FOOD

Charcuterie/Fromage Board
- Prosciutto
- Capocollo
- Brie (or better yet, Taleggio or Mont Briac if you can find it)
- Aged Cheddar Cheese
- Gouda Cheese
- Apples, Grapes, and Strawberries
- Marcona Almonds
- Chocolate covered peanuts or almonds

DRINK

- Hot Chocolate (Natasha's favorite)
- Wine for the guests
- Sparkling Water

AMBIANCE

- Low lighting and a few candles burning.
- Music playing in the background the moment guests arrive.

Natasha's favorites
- Tuck & Patti
- The Police
- Bonnie Raitt
- Shawn Colvin
- Phil Collins/Genesis
- Allen Stone

Gather everyone in a circle at a table or in a large space like a living room and have a blast talking through everyone's experience with the book. Use the following questions to spur conversation and share your discoveries and insights.

BOOK CLUB QUESTIONS

1. What are your thoughts on the opening sentence of the book (the Prelude)?

2. How do you think life would have been different for Natasha if she never discovered the violin?

3. Were there any points in the book that were unexpectedly emotional for you? What were they? How do you feel about Natasha's dad taking her to the homeless shelter?

4. Were you surprised to learn that Natasha stayed close to her father and her brothers?

5. In what ways are you able to relate to Natasha's life?

6. Which time in Natasha's life is most memorable to you and why?

7. How did this book make you feel?

8. What did you find inspiring about this book?

9. Has reading *Relentless* changed you in any way? If so, how?

10. Share a favorite quote from the book. Why does this stand out to you?

11. Is there anything you wish Natasha would have elaborated on? What would it be and why?

12. If you could share *Relentless* with one person, who would it be and why?

13. If you could ask Natasha one thing, what would it be?

CPSIA information can be obtained
at www.ICGtesting.com
Printed in the USA
LVHW011138230322
714108LV00015B/1096